TALES OF
LONDON'S
DOCKLANDS

TALES OF
LONDON'S
DOCKLANDS

HENRY T. BRADFORD

SUTTON PUBLISHING

First published in 2007 by
Sutton Publishing Limited · Phoenix Mill
Thrupp · Stroud · Gloucestershire · GL5 2BU

British Library Cataloguing in Publication Data
A catalogue record for this book is available from the British Library

ISBN 978-0-7509-4138-9

Half Title Page: The *Zealandia*, formerly *Empire Winnie*, in Gravesend
Reach, 1946. *(Author's collection)*

Title Page: Wapping Basin, June 1960. *(Tower Hamlets Local History Library)*

Typeset in Ehrhardt.
Typesetting and origination by
Sutton Publishing Limited.
Printed and bound in England by
J.H. Haynes & Co. Ltd, Sparkford.

CONTENTS

East India Docks gateway, *c*. 1945. *(Whiffin photograph collection)*

FOREWORD

One of the delights and privileges of being a general practitioner is that of getting a glimpse into other people's way of life. In the late 1970s, I was taken on a working visit to Tilbury Docks by the author of this book, just as the docks were in transition between the old ways of working and the new.

There was, inside the perimeter fence, a chain-link fence that cut the dock in half, on one side of which there were pale-faced, miserable-looking men, towing containers around on carriers, and on the other side were rumbustious, red-faced men, standing around and arguing between frenzied bouts of physical action. I was invited to help load bags of cement onto rope slings from high piles in a barge, so that they could be hoisted aboard ship, and soon learned the back-breaking nature of the work.

Best of all, I learned something of being a citizen of that closed male world, inside the walls and gates, where the dangerous nature of the work imposed its own discipline and where mutual support and cooperation were essential to avoid serious injury, or even death.

In the old days, each hatch on a ship would have a gang of twelve or thirteen men to load or discharge it, and these gangs became like alternative families, in which each member, utterly to my surprise, had gained expertise in some unexpected pursuit, such as playing chess, bridge, mending sewing machines, studying Greek mythology or interesting themselves in philately or as numismatists.

Most of the men had left school young (at 14 years of age) and served in the war, and possibly because of this there was constant arguing, intellectual ferment and a desire by many of them to learn. If anyone was sick or injured, the other gang members would cover for him within the limit of their powers. This chivalrous behaviour had to go, of course, in the perpetual drive towards 'greater productivity', and the gang system was broken up.

It has all gone now: the excitement and drama are no more; no one will tickle the back of your neck with a crane hook, just for the fun of it. The containers have won. That, as they say, is progress.

Dr Colin Smith
February 2007

ABOUT THE AUTHOR

Henry T. Bradford was born in Gravesend, Kent, in October 1930. His father had been a regular soldier in the Royal West Kent Regiment before and during the First World War, serving in the trenches till he was wounded in the battle of the Somme. Mr Bradford met Henry's mother, Eliza Reynolds, in Aldershot. They were married in the village church in Pebmarsh, Essex, and settled in Gravesend, where they had nine children, Henry being the eighth.

As a child Henry had a sparse, primitive education because of poor teaching methods and because he was evacuated during the Second World War, once to Dereham, Norfolk, in September 1939, then to Totnes, Devon, in June 1940. In Devon he was injured in a farm accident and this necessitated his spending a year in Torbay hospital and Exeter orthopaedic hospital before being returned home to Gravesend, disabled for life.

Soldiers of G. Company, 1st Battalion Queen's Own Royal West Kent Regiment, resting after having been in the front line for nineteen days, *c.* 1916. *(Author's collection)*

The ten last remaining soldiers of G. Company, 1st Battalion, Queen's Own Royal West Kent Regiment, after taking Hill 60, April 1915, France. *(Author's collection)*

After leaving school in September 1944, Henry was employed in numerous jobs before following his father into the port transport industry in March 1954 as a registered dock worker. Then, having been severely injured in a shipboard accident in April 1960, Henry attended night classes for two years before applying and being accepted on a post-graduate diploma course at the London School of Economics and Political Science. After graduation, he returned to the docks, where, during 1964–5, he wrote a comprehensive labour plan for the permanent employment of all registered dock workers.

Henry was married in December 1955 to Iris Kathleen Mann. They had two children, Dawn and Roland. Henry retired from the port transport industry in December 1986 on account of injuries sustained in dock accidents. He had spent thirty-four years employed in the industry, working in every conceivable job both on the docks and in clerical work. After retiring, Henry was advised by a literary friend that he should write stories about his experiences and vast knowledge of the docklands. Except for a story called 'Those Revolting Animals' and some short pieces, his memories appear in print only here, and can best be described as historical tales of dock work in the middle of the twentieth century.

Philip Connolly
September 2006

ACKNOWLEDGEMENTS

I would like to take this opportunity to thank the following family and friends for coaxing me into writing this book of stories and making it possible for me to do so. Foremost among them are my former workmates in the Port of London, men with whom I worked in the docks, on the wharfs and deepwater anchorages on the River Thames, dockers and stevedores, OST clerks and ships clerks, Freemen of the River, lightermen, bargemen, tugboat men and lock gatekeepers. Without their wit, humour and shenanigans, strength and skills, and in some circumstances their courage, these stories could never have been written.

Then, of course, there were the mobile canteen tea ladies. What would we have done without their sometimes cynical comments and rapturous laughter – especially when they saw us plastered in cement dust, moving towards them as if we were concrete statues, or when we were covered in Rhodesian blue or Canadian white asbestos fibres that gave us the appearance of being large lumps of mouldy cheese, or plastered all over with carbon black or red or yellow ochre powder, or stinking to high heaven of fish meal, or reeking from the stench of a cargo of wet animal skins. Even I have been known to blush at some of their witticism.

Then there is Mrs Denise Leppard, without whom these stories wouldn't have been written; Mrs Christine Morrad, who has read through them; and the late Daniel John Foley MBE JP, the venerable Welfare Officer of Sector 3, Dock Labour Compound, the London Dock Labour Board, Tilbury Docks. He was my friend and mentor without whose gentle, forceful and persistent persuasion I should never have received the further education necessary for me to be capable of compiling these stories. The late Mr J.B. Allen, the Principal Education Officer at the Adult Education Centre, New Road, Chatham, understood my reluctance to attend adult education classes because of my semi-literacy. He gave me separate lessons and the confidence to carry on with my studies – a wise and good friend. The late Keith Thurley (Professor of Industrial Relations and Personnel Management) was my very extraordinary, patient and ultra-academic tutor at the London School of Economics and Political Science. I often sought his wise counsel. Mr Philip Connolly, my shrewd and knowledgeable friend, watches over my work and was responsible for the publication of a book of my poems.

Then lastly, but most importantly, I must thank my wife, Iris Kathleen, whose patience with me is quite simply beyond belief. She has nursed me through numerous accidents and tends to my injuries still. What more could one ask of anyone? Bless her.

INTRODUCTION

It is difficult for me to know where to start with these *Tales of London's Docklands*. The period covered in this book is 1954 to 1960 when a shipboard accident put an end to my active days as a docker crane driver. Arguably the tales should begin when I was a child, not really knowing what ports, docks, dockers and stevedores were or what they represented. Nor was I any the wiser as to what was meant by certain snippets of conversations that took place in our home.

The first major clue to my father's occupation came when I was 7 years of age and attended Church Street School, Gravesend. The school overlooked the Thames and Tilbury Docks on the far shore. The schoolmaster was looking across the river. Without turning to face the class he said: 'Henry! Your father is a stevedore, isn't he?' (He always called a boy by his Christian name when he was in the mood to cane him.)

'No, sir,' I replied. 'I don't think so, sir. He's a docker, sir.'

'I said,' he repeated, 'your father is a stevedore, isn't he, Henry?'

Because I was ignorant as to the difference between a docker and stevedore, and had no particular wish to get thrashed, I simply replied, 'Yes, sir!' The master turned and faced the class, 'Yes, sir!' he repeated, 'and one day *you* shall all be working over there' (the *you* bit meant he was referring to the whole class), 'for *you* are what is generally known in polite society as nonentities.'

As I lived with my family on a council estate, I had already learned what was meant by polite society, but not about 'nonentities'. At the time his snide remark went over my head, but I had already discovered that polite society was about as polite as most civil servants were civil to people they considered to be beneath them.

Some twenty-five years later, when I was a student at the London School of Economics and Political Science, I happened to be reading through the Education Acts (that's the sort of thing one is expected to do when being schooled at such a grandiose institute) when I suddenly remembered that word, 'nonentities', and reflected on what the schoolmaster had said. Then I realized why all the lads in my form at the secondary school I had been obliged to attend were consigned to remain in the 'lower classes' for ever. We were the sons of dockers, stevedores, coal porters and other groups of men who worked in the docks, on the river or in associated employment, and of course the unemployed were included in this lowly social group. We were, you see, the children whose parents were not in 'full-time remunerative employment'. That, then, was the reason why we, the children of the river, were not allowed to sit the eleven-plus examination for a place at the grammar school. I suppose, therefore, that short bit of verbal enlightenment from the schoolmaster was the closest I ever came as a child to finding out where my father was employed, or what it was to mean to me in later life.

Not that we children ever saw much of our father. This was because he left the house each morning long before we younger ones were got up for school (my elder sisters had left school and were working by the time my memory of that period came to life), and more often than not he arrived back home after we were put to bed. Sometimes he would not come in till the next day if a ship was due to sail on the morning's early tide. Then he would be required to work day and night to complete its loading or discharging operation. This was because he was a 'perm', a permanently employed docker for a stevedoring company, paid a monthly guaranteed full back-wage. As such, he was committed to fulfil that guarantee by working day and night if he 'fell into debt', that is if he had not earned enough money within the month to repay the monthly guarantee to his employer.

Perms were physically burned-out human shells by the time they reached 40 years of age. One old docker once told me he had been called before a stevedoring contractors manager one day and informed that his services were no longer required. When he asked why, he was told, 'We've had your steel. Now you can take your old iron somewhere else.' This was a typical employer's attitude. Labour was cheap and abundant. Dozens of men were waiting for every available job. The situation was simply any employer's dream.

I did notice each day when I got up to go to school that one of the docker's hooks that had hung on the copper-pipe picture rail in our living room the evening before was missing. I should have been able to determine what sort of cargo my father was working that day by the type of hook missing from the picture rail. But it was to be many years before I came to learn that lesson the hard way.

Each hook was different from the others. One was short handled for use on general cargo, in other words packages, cases and cartons. These contained anything from cars to cocoa powder, ammunition, bristles, carbon black and such like. Another was a pad hook (an oval-shaped thick steel plate with short spikes on its surface designed to grip sacks and not to penetrate into the contents) to be used in bag work – for example, sacks of asbestos, cocoa beans or dried blood. The third was a bag hook (a short-handled tool with two hooks), also used for bag work where contents would not be damaged by the use of a hook. The fourth was a long-handled hook for use on wet or dry wood pulp. Wood pulp was imported in bales, mainly from the Scandinavian countries, Russia and Canada; it was bound in wire straps, and each bale weighed 3–4 hundredweight.

Hooks were essential tools in the docks. They gave the user an extended arm and also extra leverage in moving cargo. They were also dangerous as weapons. Other equipment, such as shovels, ropes and wires, cargo nets, ore baskets, loading boards and running boards, was provided by the shipping line or the stevedoring contractor, that is the company contracted to service the ship. However, mechanical appliances such as quay cranes and mobile cranes, used in transit sheds and warehouses, were invariably the property of the Port Authority. There were exceptions, for example, electrically operated trucks. When these were used they would be charged against a gang's earnings as an extra man on the daily 'tick note'. In other words, the gang actually paid to hire the truck from the employer.

Another childhood memory that sticks in my mind is the pungent smell of camphorated oil. My mother used to massage my father's back with it when he came home exhausted after having worked the clock round. She would then crack and whisk two raw eggs into a glass of milk and he would drink it. He then went to bed for several hours, got up, washed and shaved, dressed, had a meal and made his way to one of the allotments he kept. He would spend several hours digging and planting seeds to produce crops for his family, then come home to get ready to return to the docks and more work.

There were eleven in our family including Mum and Dad. We children were three boys and six girls. Between the First and Second World Wars millions of people were unemployed and their families were starving. That did not happen to my family. This was entirely due to my father's hard work. He spent forty-seven years in the docks with one good hand – the other had been shot through in the battle of the Somme.

Those, of course, were the good old days. My father was obliged to retire from the docks on his 68th birthday in 1965. He found himself another job and worked on till he was 73 before finally retiring. He died in his 87th year. He was

Main gate of the London Dock. (Industries of Stepney, *Metropolitan Borough of Stepney, 1948*)

physically and mentally worn out by hard work, war wounds (both physical and mental) and injuries he had sustained in the docks.

For my part, I entered the port transport industry as a registered dock worker in April 1954, through the good offices of the Port of London Authority. I was entered on the Port Authority 'A' list, a preference list of dockers who were called off for work by the authority's labour master and allocated to specific jobs throughout the docks. I left the Port Authority when a traffic officer in charge of a job I was working on refused to pay dirty-handling money on asbestos. (That was before asbestos was recognized as a dangerous substance.) I then went on 'the free call' for employment with the stevedoring labour contractors.

The people I worked with in the docks were all ex-servicemen, men who had been involved in battles wherever battles had been fought by British forces during conflicts that went back as far as the South African War at the end of the nineteenth century. Others had served in the two world wars or had been involved in battles fought in India, Persia and Palestine between 1918 and 1939. The Malayan Emergency, Korean War, Cyprus, Kenya and Suez were yet to come for many of those released from military service on the 'Z' Reserve List. They were hard, tough men with phenomenal stamina and a bloody-minded sense of humour. They looked after their own people at work just as they had had to look after each other in the services. When they took part in sports, they played as hard as they worked. It was a great honour and privilege to have known them and been accepted on equal terms by them.

My first morning's work as a docker was to whitewash quayside bollards. At midday I was paid off and returned to the Dock Labour Board compound for the afternoon muster. Then I was sent to a job removing 4-hundredweight drums of arsenic from rail trucks. My brother was the ganger and welcomed me with: 'Ah! Henry, you've run into a bit of luck. We've got 250 tons to strike out of open rail trucks. If we get the job finished by half past four we may be transferred to the next shed and get two hours' overtime striking freight off lorries.'

My brother made sure we finished the job by half past four, and we did transfer to the adjoining shed and worked till 7 p.m. We hoisted our tonnage to 400 tons that afternoon. In those days the Port Authority piecework rate was 2s 6d per deadweight ton per eight-handed gang or two-fifths measurement, whichever was the greater, or so we were led to believe. That was 3d 3 farthings per man for each ton of cargo handled. Not too bad for a first afternoon; I wasn't to be that lucky again for several years.

The tales that follow are still vivid in my memory, more than four decades after the accident that took me away from working on the docks. They are colourful glimpses of a world long since disappeared. However, to save any possible embarrassment to relatives or friends, the names of the characters who appear in these pages have been changed.

1
DOCKERS OR FILM STARS?

Eric was a year younger than me. Although we had been to the same school in Gravesend and I had encountered him as a boy, we came from different areas within the Borough and never got to know each other for two specific reasons. First, his father was a shipwright, employed by a ship repair company that operated within Tilbury Docks and on vessels on the River Thames. He was therefore classed as an artisan in full-time remunerative employment. This meant Eric was prime candidate for the A and B forms when we were at school. The second reason we didn't get to know each other was that I was a docker's son. Dockers were not considered to be in full-time remunerative employment, as they were subject to the vagaries of shipping cycles. That meant there were possibly periods when they were obliged to sign on the dole. So, I, my father's youngest son, languished in C forms until my last term at school when I reached the pinnacle of my academic career, as it then stood, by being elevated as a senior schoolboy into Form 4, the top class. But this was undoubtedly due to a change in national policy under the Education Act of 1944, rather than to the intentions of county authority education policy or of the school staff, who had been totally indoctrinated by previous statutes, which were designed to provide a minimum level of education for the children of the labouring classes.

When I left school, I had a variety of jobs before entering the docklands of the Port of London. Eric, however, had been sent to train as a chef in the Grosvenor Hotel, London. Of course, I had failed my medical for conscripted military service on account of an injury sustained during the war when I was an evacuee; it had left me with a stiff leg. Eric, on the other hand, had passed his medical with flying colours and been selected for service with the Royal Navy. During his national service he had volunteered to join one of the naval gun teams that take part in the military displays at the Royal Tournament. Unfortunately, he had fractured his skull during practice and had had to be invalided out of the service.

Eric came to work in the docks shortly after me and we often worked together. He had grown from being a skinny, lanky boy at school into a 6-foot 3-inch man with dark, Italianate features. Women found him to be handsome, so he had no trouble picking up girlfriends. He was also articulate in his speech and suave in deportment. He used his hands to explain things, just like Frenchmen tend to do.

He should have been a salesman; he would have been able to sell refrigerators to Eskimos living in the Arctic Circle or electric fires to Africans living on the Equator. I was about 6 feet tall and a good bit broader than Eric, but had nowhere near his obvious handsome features and inherent charm. So, naturally, people spoke to him rather than to me.

Now, I have to admit, we younger men were a bit rebellious both in the docks and outside. The reason for this was, unlike our fathers and grandfathers, we had been educated up to the three Rs level and had a modicum of an idea we were human beings. Therefore we were averse to being treated as brainless beasts of burden by port employers in the docks and as social lepers outside. The reception we received was caused exclusively by adverse propaganda encouraged by consecutive governments, port employers and the media press barons, who were always looking for scapegoats to take the pressure off, or to divert attention away from, government political blunders or employers' industrial misdeeds. We also resented being cheated out of some of our piecework earnings. Payments were due to us for tonnages of cargo loaded or discharged from ships, and day-work money for quay operations was being withheld by shed foremen and ship's charge clerks. In addition, ship workers failed to pay us for lost time for day-work done outside piecework operations. Of course those people were umbrageous at being challenged about their integrity, or lack of it, and when dissenters such as us offered our services to them on the free call, none of the ship workers or quay foremen would give us a job if they could possibly avoid doing so. In consequence, we were forever left 'on the stones' (unemployed) or were sent out of sector (our designated docks) to other docks within the Port of London or even to another port.

Now, in order to overcome this problem, I had to think which jobs were the most important within the industry. After watching the ship workers who were left on the call stands waiting for men, I concluded that crane drivers and winch drivers were the kingpins on which everyone relied: without crane drivers it was almost impossible to do any work aboard ships in the enclosed docks, and without winch drivers no work could be done afloat on the river. It was, therefore, imperative that, to get a job in the docks, Eric and I had to get a crane driver's licence.

I must point out that it was not easy to get a licence to drive Port Authority quay cranes. There was a whole gambit of regulations and procedures to go through. One had to find a sponsor among the employers, be examined by the Port Authority's medical officer and passed grade 1 fit. Then one had to undergo a strenuous three weeks of training sessions under the tutelage and supervision of expert crane drivers employed by shipping companies or labour contractors. Then one had to be passed out as competent to drive any of the various types of crane owned and operated by the Port Authority. Competence-testing for crane drivers was carried out by the chief mechanical and electrical engineers, who were responsible for, and in charge of, all Port of London Authority mechanical appliances.

In my endeavour to obtain a crane driver's licence I went to see the manager of Maltby's Stevedoring Company in Tilbury Docks. He was a big man in every sense of the word. But, unlike most of his contemporaries in the stevedoring business, he was reasonably intelligent. He had, unlike them, been educated at a

Wapping Basin, June 1960. *(Tower Hamlets Local History Library)*

public school and an Oxford college, and it was rumoured he had a university blue in boxing, but this was probably a story put about to intimidate those mortals with little faith in their own fighting abilities. (If so, he was on a loser there, because I wasn't aware of anyone in the docks who couldn't fight in those days, especially in London, where all schools had physical education teachers who taught boxing as part of the curriculum, as did all the boys' clubs in and around the capital.) He had served as a colonel in the Royal Engineers, Docks Battalion during the Second World War, an experience that quite possibly expanded his knowledge of our peasant society, but which had also made him a bit of an authoritarian. Yet, even with the flaws in his social and educational background, he was not averse to reasoned and intelligent argument and persuasion. It certainly wasn't too difficult to acknowledge that he was more of a gentleman than the rest of the stevedoring and shipping line company managers, even if he did speak as though he had a plum in his mouth and smoked an old cherry wood pipe.

Maltby's office was in Tenants Road, Tilbury Docks. There I was greeted with, 'What do you want?' by a pale-faced clerk who was sitting on a high stool at a high desk in a small dingy outer office – an office that was reminiscent of Scrooge's counting house in Charles Dickens's *A Christmas Carol*.

'I want to see your governor!' I replied. (All managers of shipping and labour contracting companies that operated in the docks were called governor. It was by force of habit one referred to them as such.)

'What for?' he asked.

I said, 'Just tell him the Dock Labour Board manager has sent me to see him.' (He hadn't, of course, but the office clerk didn't know that.)

That got the pale-faced youth mobile. He slid off his seat with dexterity and verve to rap sharply on an adjoining door that was marked with the designation in large letters, 'THE GOVERNOR'S OFFICE', under which some wag had written in letters not much larger than the small print on a written guarantee the words, 'THE BUCK STOPS HERE'. He went in. He quickly came out and gestured me to go in. I was shown into a large, well-lit office, a complete contrast to the one outside. A swivel chair, set behind a large, long mahogany desk, revolved to face me. Very comfortably installed in it was the Governor himself, in the flesh.

'I understand the Dock Labour Board manager sent you to see me?'

'Well, sir, not in so many words, sir. I've come on my own initiative to ask if you could, sir, see your way to, sir.'

'Cut out that grovelling bullshit. It doesn't suit you. What do you want?'

'I want to obtain a Port Authority crane driver's licence.'

'How did you know I need more crane drivers?' he asked.

'Simply because your ship workers are always the last people off the call stand, and when they're asked what they're waiting for, it's always crane drivers.'

'Yes, well,' he said, 'if you can find a mate to train with you, I'll put you on a three-week training course with my crane drivers. You'll be paid the day-work rate while you're training. When you find a mate, report to the cashier in the outer office. He will make all the arrangements. Right?'

'Yes, right,' I replied.

'Clear off then,' he ordered, 'and come back and report to me when you have passed your crane driving test and you have got your licence.' That was it.

I went off and found Eric in the Tilbury Dockers' Club. I explained what had transpired between the governor of Maltby's and me. We went back to the office together and saw the cashier. He telephoned the Port of London general office and got a date for a medical examination, which was to be conducted at Trinity Square, opposite the Merchant Navy war memorial and the Tower of London.

The day of the medical examination came, and I met Eric on the Gravesend ferry terminal. We crossed the river to the Tilbury Riverside rail terminal and purchased tickets, using our dockers' rail warrant, to Fenchurch Street station. We walked from Fenchurch Street to Trinity Square and found the medical officer's surgery in the Port Authority building. We were given a through examination. I passed, even with my stiff leg, and that was a shock to Eric, because he was failed as he had varicose veins.

After the medical we left Trinity Square, looked round the Merchant Navy war memorial, and then made our way to a restaurant Eric had known when he had been a trainee chef at the Grosvenor Hotel, before his call up for national service with the Royal Navy several years before. Eric had said the prices would be a bit stiff in this restaurant, but as we were getting a travelling and subsistence

A steam ferry approaching Gravesend Riverside terminal to discharge road transport vehicles conveyed from Tilbury Riverside landing stage, 1950s. *(Author's collection)*

allowance to attend the medical examination, we could put it down to expenses. We walked in and waited to be shown to a table. A waiter came for our order. Eric said we wanted a pot of coffee and some pastries. We were quickly served and sat talking for some time, slowly drinking coffee and devouring the pastries. While we were sitting there, several different waiters came to take a look at us. I wondered what was so obviously wrong, but Eric stayed pie-faced until it was time to leave. Then he said, 'You go on, and I'll pay the bill.'

I walked a short way from the restaurant and it was several minutes before he came out with a Cheshire cat grin all over his face.

'What's so funny?' I asked.

He said, 'You may find this hard to believe, but they think you are Robert Beatty, the film actor, and I am Bonar Colleano, the film star.'

'Well! You would be the star, of course. What did you tell them?'

'I told them we were travelling incognito looking for sites to make a film. I signed a few autographs for them and promised I'd have a word with our studio director to see if he could use them when we are in the area filming.'

'And they fell for it? I don't believe you! By the way, how much were you charged for the coffee and pastries?'

'They were on the house, for as the head waiter said, "After all, we can't be seen to charge two prominent film actors who have chosen to grace our premises with their persons, now can we?"'

He pointed at me, and the stupid sod said, 'You, Robert Beatty!' and he never stopped laughing all the way home.

2

KIPPERS – HAVE A
BOX ON ME

Tilbury Docks was built for the East and West India Dock Companies. It was constructed on marshland that stretched from the Thames riverside, opposite Gravesend in Kent, to the town of Grays in Essex. The lock that allowed ships to enter and leave the docks was built to handle sailing vessels, the first coal-burning cargo ships, short sea traders, sailing barges and lighters. It was opened in 1886.

To operate the lock gates, massive pumps were used, and these had a dual purpose. They not only opened and closed the gates, but also provided power to hydraulic cranes on the quayside. These antiquated, water-powered cranes were installed in 1886 and were still being used for ship loading and discharging operations in the 1950s.

In 1928, a New Lock Entrance was constructed and opened to shipping. This allowed the largest vessels then in service to enter and leave the docks. Consequently, bigger, higher, more up-to-date electric cranes had to be installed to handle the cargo from these modern vessels. The new cranes had longer jibs for employment on overseas traders (tramp steamers) and luxury liners of the P&O and Orient lines. These ships were passenger- and cargo-carrying vessels that steamed between the Port of London, the Far East and Australia. The hydraulic cranes were therefore obsolete for use on larger ships; they were shoved to the end of the quays and to Tilbury Dock Basin (a tidal extension of Tilbury Docks open to the river) to be used for servicing short sea traders (small ships plying their trade round the coasts of Britain, Europe and the Mediterranean).

When I entered the port transport industry as a docker in 1954, hydraulic-powered cranes had been in service in Tilbury docks for seventy-eight years. The seals on the old pumping systems had worn out and not been replaced. There was a continuous shower of water spurting from them when they were in use. This only subsided when the mains valves were closed to cut off the water supply. Under Port Authority by-laws it was illegal to light an open fire within the dock precincts, or even to light or smoke cigarettes. Nonetheless, in winter, braziers were lighted under the hydraulic cranes to stop them from freezing up.

To get a hydraulic crane to operate, one had first to turn on its main water supply, which was installed under a heavy plate in the quay, then climb up a

The Zim Line m.v. *Tappuz* alongside the Nort Quay, West India Dock. *(PLA Monthly, November 1959)*

vertical 30-foot ladder into the crane cabin; then luff (move) the jib full in with a luffing lever; then climb up another ladder to release the jib by removing a securing pin; then climb back down the ladder to the front of the crane cabin to release the slewing pin. Now the crane was ready to work, with a bit of luck and with God on one's side. (At night the whole process had to be carried out in the reverse order.) These machines were a nightmare to operate and control.

Perhaps I should mention here the drill required when a ship entered the locks, the gates were closed, and the hydraulic pumps in the pumping station were put into play to fill or empty them. First, the crane driver was supposed to bring his crane round with its jib in line with the quay; he was then supposed to replace the slewing pin, luff full in and run up the ladder to replace the luffing pin; then wait for the power to be restored when the lock was filled or emptied. However, there was no signalling device to warn crane drivers of the lock master's intentions, so when the hydraulic power began to fail, the driver was forced to take any action he thought appropriate to forestall an accidents or damage to the crane or cargo, but unfortunately this could not always be avoided.

Bill Dyke was a large man. He had what the dockers called a 'beetroot' or 'moon' face because it was large, round and red. He was a jovial, lovely old man with a rustic sense of humour. He was one of the finest crane drivers in the port transport industry. That is, he was as careful, and considerate and as safe to work with as it was possible for any man to be. He never took chances with men's lives in an industry that had a horrendous number of accidental injuries and deaths. Dock working was always a dangerous game of chance.

Bill had been picked up in the Dock Labour Board compound as crane driver to a ship's gang working on a general steam short sea trader at number 5 shed, Tilbury Docks, using an antiquated hydraulic-powered quay crane to load cargo at the main hatch. Short sea traders were constructed with the bridge, crew's accommodation and engine room at the stern. This gave the crane driver good vision both of the quay and of the ship's hold. Two pairs of winches and derricks were close to midships so they could service both hatches. A mast, with a wireless aerial attached, poked up high above the bridge from between the winches.

The loading operation had gone well. The ship had finished taking on general cargo. The beams, hatches and hatch covers had been put in place and secured ready for sea. It remained only for a consignment of Scottish oakwood smoked kippers to be loaded for stowage into a cool chamber. Then the ship could cast off and sail out into the river into a golden sunset. Well, that was the theory.

The kippers had been brought down from Scotland by road. A lorry was standing on the quay. The quay gang loaded the boxes of fish onto a loading board and covered them with a cargo safety net. As most people know, boxes of kippers are quite small (about 18 inches long, 10 inches wide and 4 inches deep). There were, therefore, several hundred boxes on the set as Bill Dyke lifted it and began to slew the crane round the stern of the ship. His intention was to land the set on top of the hatches close by the cool chamber. However, fate played its hand. A ship entered the locks and the hydraulic power went off just as Bill slewed the set over the top of the funnel. As the crane lost power the set of kippers came slowly to rest on the edge of the funnel. Two of the hooks holding the cargo board came out. The boxes of kippers began to slide off the cargo board and plummet down the funnel into the engine room. The air was quickly filled with blasphemies, oaths and threats in a language that no parson within earshot would admit to understanding, let alone a bishop – well, at least not in a public place, that is.

It seemed a bit unreal at first, but everyone was soon brought back down to earth when the chief engineer, the second engineer, the donkey-man and the firemen came out of the engine room carrying boxes of kippers.

'You're supposed to put these bloody things in the cool chamber,' shouted the chief engineer to the crane driver, 'not down the engine room. What the bloody hell are we supposed to do with these?'

Bill shrugged his broad shoulders. 'Anybody hurt down there?' he asked.

'No! Lucky for you there wasn't,' the chief replied.

Bill shrugged his shoulders again and said, 'Keep a box of those kippers for the captain's tea. Tell him you've had a box or two on you, and so the crane driver said it's only fair the skipper should have a kipper or two on him.'

3

THE TEABOY'S APPRENTICE

On a cold morning in April I found myself in Tilbury Docks Labour Board compound on the look-out for a single day's work. I got picked up by a Scrutton's Stevedoring Company Limited quay foreman to work as the crane driver to a delivery gang. The gang had been allocated to load barges with chests of tea that were to be sent to the tea auction rooms at Butlers Wharf Warehouse on the South Bank of the Thames, close by London's waterfront, just below Tower Bridge.

The tea we were to deliver had been brought to Tilbury Docks from Calcutta in India and Colombo in Sri Lanka via the Suez Canal, the Mediterranean Sea,

A port health motor launch making towards a deep sea ocean trading ship as it is about to enter the River Thames, 1950s. *(Author's collection)*

the Bay of Biscay, the English Channel and the River Thames. It had come aboard the SS *Ma'hout*, a really old, worn-out vessel of the Brocklebank Line that was soon to be sent to a breakers yard to be cut up for scrap.

The trade route the SS *Ma'hout* had followed had fascinated me since I was a very small boy, and not simply because of the large number of ships that sailed along that major seaway. My father, who had been a docker since his release from the British Army after the First World War, had occasionally spoken of the varieties of freight and exotic merchandise carried by ocean trading ships, but he had talked more of the vessels that traded with countries that had once been part of the British Empire; countries that were now self-governing free states within a democratically controlled Commonwealth of Nations (a real feather, if ever there was one, in Great Britain's cap).

Among the many different shipping companies that used the London to Far Eastern and Australasian sea routes were the Pacific & Orient (P&O) and the Orient passenger- and cargo-carrying lines, Blue Funnel Line, Clan Line, Brocklebank Line, City Line and P&O cargo ships, and there were also numerous foreign-owned tramp steamers. (These are vessels that trade anywhere they can or are contracted to pick up consignments of freight; they do not run to a set schedule, as is the case with liners, and they are mainly employed on charter party terms and conditions by merchants wishing to ship bulk cargoes, or by major companies for the shipment, or trans-shipment, of small consignments of freight to ports not on their liner-specified trade routes.)

Between them, the shipping line vessels carried hundreds of thousands of tons of freight every year to and from India, Ceylon and the Far East, and to Australia, New Zealand, many ports along the East African coast and the island of Madagascar. On the outward voyage, they took with them every conceivable type of manufactured good, and quite often even the ship itself was an export, too. The vessels that traded with Far Eastern and Australasian countries bought home with them exotic cargoes of herbs and spices, ivory and wines, precious metals and gemstones, as well as all those things essential to everyday living, including tea from the gardens of Assam in northern India and Sri Lanka (formerly known as the island of Ceylon).

The men I was due to work with were a tea-delivery gang. The crane drivers to such gangs invariably worked pro rata, which meant they could be paid off when their specific task was completed. In fact this arrangement was quite often a ploy by ship workers to retain the services of their crane drivers when they were expecting a vessel to berth: no work aboard ship could be carried out without crane drivers' or winch drivers' expert knowledge.

Quay delivery gangs comprised twelve men: two barge hands, two pitch hands, two men to load the wheelbarrows and six wheelbarrow men to push the tea chests from the transit shed onto the quay. There they were placed onto a cargo board or a tea board to be lifted or slid into the stowage bay of a barge. When the time came to make tea for the gang, one of the wheelbarrow men was delegated to carry out this task, and that obviously reduced their number to five, with the subsequent loss of two chests of tea on each run from the tea beds in the transit sheds to the pitch on the quay. During the course of a single day this could amount to 100 chests of tea, and at the time of this tale, the piecework rate was £1 5s 5d per hundred chests of tea. Divided between twelve men, this was equal to 25½d per man per day. It was general practice for the wheelbarrow men to carry two, and sometimes three, chests (each weighing approximately 140 pounds) from the tea beds in a transit shed to their stowage, and this was more especially so if the gangs had a long walk between the shed and the lighter or barge that would be berthed alongside the dock quay.

The daily productivity target for the tea-delivery gangs, set by the men themselves, was 300 chests of tea per man, to be moved from the transit shed into a barge between 8 a.m. and 7 p.m., 3,600 chests of tea a day. As a result, they were very keen to press the pro-rata man into making the tea.

I had been standing in the crane cabin after removing the stern beam of a barge, waiting to hoist the first half-dozen sets of tea from the quay pitch by cargo board into the stern bay of an empty craft. There were no seats in any of the cranes, unless the driver struggled up three separate 20-foot vertical steel ladders with an old orange box or some other suitable packing case. We dockers invariably worked a ten-hour day, so you might think that providing a seat for the crane operators would not have been beyond the financial capability of the vehicles' owners, but the Port Authority would not be persuaded that, even from an ergonomics point of view, seats should be installed in the 80-foot high-flying cranes. For, it was strongly emphasized by management, the Port Authority could not afford the cost of putting seats in cranes. However, it did not go unnoticed by the crane drivers that Port Authority administrative staff were not required to stand at their desks for their seven-hour day, five-day week.

One sometimes wondered what was in the minds of the people who had been given responsibility for running the busiest port on this earth. After all, it could not have been business acumen, because management always appeared, to me at least, to be totally devoid of any business sense at all. Therefore, one had to ask oneself, was it some idiotic form of class prejudice that dictated management policies, especially as they related to the lack of the most basic facilities. These decisions and policies brought about inefficiencies in work practices and physical discomfort because of the lack of welfare amenities for all workers, particularly those dockers and stevedores employed as casual labour by shipping lines and stevedoring contractors. Was this the result of class prejudice? Who can tell. But if it was, I find it extraordinary that such petty-mindedness and childish snobbery from even the lowest members of Port Authority staff should have been allowed to stand in the way of the port's industrial progress. The truth of the matter is that the responsibility for such industrial arrogance in labour relations and mean-mindedness in welfare provisions stemmed from the policies emanating from the Port of London Board, an authority set up in 1908 to administer all the docks in the Port of London (with the exception of the Regent's Canal Dock), their wharves, warehouses and transit sheds, policing and river dredging. But here comes the crunch: the Port Authority Board, which was principally made up of ship owners, barge and lighterage owners and merchants, also had two trade union representatives to voice the interests of dock workers. It has never been recorded that they ever served any useful purpose as far as port workers were concerned.

However, I digress from the story of the tea. The operation of putting the first two tiers of tea chests into a lighter or barge with the aid of a crane was called flooring out, as it raised the floor of the stowage by about 2 feet 6 inches per tier, after which the gang would use tea boards (short wooden boards with strong wooden blocks attached to them at one end that hooked onto the edge of a lighter or barge combing). This sped up the delivery operation simply because the barrowmen released their load directly onto the tea board. This cut out the need for the crane and temporarily made the crane driver surplus to requirements. Therefore, when flooring out was achieved, I was nominated teaboy for the morning break.

Charley C. was well into his fifties. He was short and stocky and as physically fit as any man half his age could be. He had been a regular soldier before and during the war, first in the Essex Regiment, after which he had transferred into an Army Commando unit. Charley had a mind like a razor, and knew every trick in survival techniques you could think of, plus a lot more besides. Charley didn't suffer fools gladly, as I was soon to find out when the ganger asked me if I would make the tea. Like a fool, I agreed. 'See Charley. He'll tell you what to do.'

Charley was busily in transit, almost running, with two chests of tea on his wheelbarrow. 'I can't stop,' he called out. 'The tea box and stores are in the cooper's workshop. Get the hot water out of the Port Authority foreman's office.'

I waved to let him know I understood, and set about my task. When I opened the tea box it contained thirteen mugs, three large tins of Libby's milk, and a 2-pound bag of Tate & Lyle sugar, but no tea. I did no more, but got on my bicycle and rode out to the local general store to buy a quarter-pound packet of tea. I quickly returned to the transit shed with my purchase. It was getting near tea-up time, so I got more than a few dirty looks from the gang as I rode past them. I retrieved their battered old aluminium, gallon-sized teapot from the cooper's workshop and went into the shed foreman's office to get some hot water. I put about 2 ounces of tea into the pot and poured water from a wall-mounted heater onto the leaves before returning to the cooper's shop. As I left his office, the PLA shed foreman gave me a quizzical look, as though he thought I was either stupid or mad, but he said not a word. I wasn't to realize till later that I had broken a golden rule. I simply walked back into the transit shed where the gang had rigged up a table with some tea chests and cheerfully called out, 'Tea-up!'

As each man emptied his wheelbarrow onto the tea board at the barge he made his way to the cooper's workshop, picked up a mug and filled it with tea, took a mouthful, spat it out and cried out.

'Gowd help us! What the bloody hell is this?' or words to that effect came from all directions.

'What's wrong?' I asked in all innocence.

'This isn't bloody tea. It's mouthwash. Where did you get it?'

'There wasn't any tea in the tea box so I went to the shop outside and bought some.'

'You did what?' Charley cried out in despair. He began to wave his hand up and down the transit shed.

'What do you think is in these chests? Why do you think they are called tea chests? No, then let me surprise you. It's because they're full of tea-leaves. We can't work all day on this rubbish. It's what office workers drink.' Then turning round to face the other members of the tea-delivery gang, he said, 'You lads go back to work and I'll teach him', he waved his finger at me, 'how to make a real cup of tea. I'll give you a shout when I've made a fresh cup.'

The gang, still mumbling all sorts of vile and violent threats against my person, continued their tirade till confidence could be restored by the production of the genuine substance as brewed by Charley, who should have been crowned 'King of the Tilbury Docks Teaboys'.

'Now,' said Charley, giving me my first lesson, 'this is our tea caddy in which we keep our loose tea-leaves.' He produced a large tin from behind a pile of chests. 'These', he said as he spread a hand around the transit shed which held thousands of chests of tea, 'are tea chests. Each tea chest has a number marked on it and that number indicates which tea garden it came from. Now, when we ship these chests of tea to the auction rooms, buyers from different companies purchase them by the tea garden mark. Then they are sent to a tea tasters' laboratory, where the different teas are brewed. Tea tasters, or whatsoever they may call themselves, then take a mouthful of each different brew, swill it about in their mouths, spit it out, wash their mouths out with fresh water, and then taste the next brew, and so on. The idea is that retailers may continue to sell the same-tasting product, such as Brooke Bond Divided Tea, Tetley's Tea, and the various teas sold by the Co-op retail grocery shops.

'Well, we haven't got time to sod about doing that so what we do is: take two handfuls of tea-leaves from chests marked numbers 1 and 7; four handfuls from chests marked 3 and 10 – those teas, by the way, come from Assam tea gardens and other north Indian tea plantations; then we need a couple of handfuls of number 21 from Sri Lanka. Now, notice how I shove my hand to the bottom of the tea caddy and stir all the different teas. That's my way of blending it. Right! That's it. That will do. Our next job is to get the water. Come on,' he said, 'follow me.'

He led me back into the Port Authority shed foreman's office. 'Sorry about this, Gov,' he pointed at me. 'He made a cock-up just now with making the tea. I've got to make a fresh pot.'

Charley took a sixpence from his pocket and placed it in a battered old Oxo tin that had a hole punched in the top, watched very closely by the Gov.

'That's the second pot you've had this morning,' said the Gov.

'Didn't he pay when he came in earlier?' said Charley.

I butted in. 'I wasn't aware we had to pay for the water. I bought the tea, you know.'

Both of them looked at me as if I was raving mad. Charley said, 'We know you bought some tea, you idiot. Now for Christ's sake just put another sixpence in the tea kitty or we won't get a cup of tea this morning.' I did as I was bid.

We made our way back to the shed and the cooper's shop. Charley opened a tin of Libby's evaporated milk and poured the whole lot into the teapot, then added a mug of Tate & Lyle sugar. He stirred the lot together with a piece of wood, then called, 'Beer-oh.'

Loading bales of sheepskins onto a lighter. *(The Sport and General Press*

The barrows went to the ground, tea chests and all, as the gang hurried to get their first drink for three hours. They sat sipping the brew with relish and I have to admit it was the finest cup of tea I had ever tasted.

'Well, son,' said Charley, 'what do you think of that? Now that's a cup of tea, isn't it?'

'Marvellous!' I had to admit. 'Marvellous!'

'Then there ends your first tea-making lesson,' Charley said. 'Now you can go back up in the crane and do what you're best at. The lighterman is waiting for you to put the barge beam back on.'

So I did.

4
BIG DAVE AND THE
FERRY BOAT INCIDENT

He was known as Big Dave for one simple reason: he was big. But he was also immensely strong. Some of the dockers who knew him well, and worked with him quite often, said he was as strong as a horse, and I, for one, wouldn't doubt it. Big Dave was an easy-going, genial bloke, but he was not a person to be put upon, or to be made a fool of either. No one had ever seen him really upset, but it had to be assumed he could get very nasty if agitated.

He was 6 feet 6 inches tall, broad in the shoulders and weighed 25 stone. You would not think anyone in their right mind would ever be so rash or foolish as to rub him up the wrong way, not a giant like Big Dave. But I would not be telling you the truth if I were to say such things never happened to that benign and lovable man, because they did.

Tilbury-to-Gravesend steam ferry in mid-river with passengers, 1950s. *(Author's collection)*

Gravesend-to-Tilbury steam ferry loading vehicles to be conveyed to Tilbury Riverside landing stage, 1950s. *(Author's collection)*

Big Dave, like hundreds of other men who worked in the docks, crossed the River Thames each day from Gravesend to the Tilbury landing stage by the steam ferry. Many of the ferry passengers were artisans and labourers who worked for ship repair companies in the docks, while most of the others were dockers, making their way to the call stands in the Dock Labour Board compound in the hope of finding employment on the free call – or free-for-all as it was more commonly known to the registered dockers. Another group of ferry passengers were permanently employed dockers, that is registered dockers who were full-time employees of the Port of London Authority or of labour contractors to the shipping lines.

Five ferries sailed back and forth from Gravesend to Tilbury each day, two passenger vessels and three carrying vehicles. The passenger boats left every quarter-hour, the vehicle boats every half-hour. This meant that, if passengers missed one ferry, they could hurry round to the other terminal and catch the next boat.

Big Dave always caught the vehicle ferry because he rode a bicycle to work. It had been a police bicycle and it had 26½-inch wheels – a big, upright, hard-wearing bicycle, built to carry a heavyweight police officer. It could just about manage Big Dave's huge weight.

Big Dave rode his bicycle to work every day, summer and winter, rain, snow or shine, and he always caught the 7.30 ferry boat. On the day of this tale, the vehicle ferry was loading cars. Small vehicles were placed in the bow and stern spaces so that the larger ones, such as coaches and lorries, could be driven straight onto and off the vessels when they berthed on the Riverside passenger jetty on the opposite side of the Thames.

Big Dave was walking along the driveway towards the ferry entrance, pushing his bicycle, keeping up with the car in front of him. The car driver coming up behind him was in a Morris convertible. There was not much of the driver to be seen, except for his shoulders and his head, which was large, round and bald. He had a handlebar moustache, which gave people the impression he had served in the Royal Air Force during the Second World War, he was wearing steel-rimmed glasses, and he was smoking a pipe. Unfortunately, he was driving faster than the people in front of him and he struck the back of Big Dave's bicycle.

Big Dave looked round, then down to the rear of his cycle. There was no apparent damage. He then looked up at the driver, who stared at him for several seconds. The man raised his right arm in front of him with his fingers pointed downwards; he raised them twice towards Big Dave, intimating to him to get out of the way.

Big Dave slowly placed his cycle against the wall of the ferry cashier's office, purposely blocking the roadway to stop the driver from passing him. Then he turned round and lifted the front of the offender's car up to hip height before letting it drop to the ground. The car driver's pipe flew from his mouth, his steel-rimmed glasses fell down over his nose, and his head struck the windscreen. When he looked up he saw Big Dave staring down at him. The Big Man was showing no sign of emotion whatsoever. He put up his hand and waved his index finger at the car driver, winked his eye, turned round and retrieved his cycle.

Passengers aboard a Tilbury-to-Gravesend steam ferry approaching Gravesend town pier in the 1950s. (*Author's collection*)

Charabancs on Tilbury Riverside Passenger Terminal waiting to board a vehicle and passenger steam ferry to Gravesend, 1950s. *(Author's collection)*

Then he calmly walked off down the vehicle ramp towards the ferry boat. The car driver wound down his window and, in a hurt tone of voice, said to one of the dockers making towards the ferry entrance, 'I say, old chap, did you see what he did to my car?'

'Yes,' replied the docker, 'and it must be your lucky day. I've seen him turn cars like yours upside down. Wait till I tell the lads at work. They'll all have a good laugh.' Then, as though it were an afterthought, he said, 'But I suppose the reason he let you off was he didn't want to hold the ferry up and make us all late for work. You really were very lucky, you know'. Then, with as much sarcasm as it was possible to muster, he barked out, 'Old chap' He then bent down, leaned into the car window and said in a very low voice, 'You should be more careful in future. You never know who you might be bumping into next, do you?'

5

BIG DAVE AND THE FORMER YEOMAN OF SIGNALS

S o we sat there, on the bollards of the foredeck of the SS *Iberia*, and waited for the ship's passengers to arrive as the thick fog, which was slowly thinning hour by hour, swirled about us. A watery sun was distinctly beginning to show itself through the fog layer that covered the river from shore to shore as far as the eye could see, say about 300 feet, but certainly not more.

Gangs of dockers had completed loading the ship's cargo the previous day; all the steel deck hatch lid covers had been lowered and bolted down; the derricks had been replaced by the Lascar deckhands into the appropriate crutches and secured ready for the ship to go to sea. Baggage gangs, working on the quayside, were transporting suitcases and travelling trunks of personal effects (that is, the luggage that would be required by passengers en route to their destinations in Sri Lanka and Australia) from private cars and taxis that had been drawn up against a raised platform at the rear of the transit shed. Those arriving were, of course, first-class passengers in the main.

There was neither sight nor sound of a British Railways steam train that was to bring most of the tourist-class passengers to the ship from London's Fenchurch Street station. We dockers who made up the ship's baggage gang had to wait out on the open deck as the fog swirled round us. It enmeshed us, like silkworms in their cocoons, as droplets of water formed on our eyebrows and soaked our clothing through to our skins. There was nowhere to shelter, and the doors to the forward lounge were kept locked to make quite sure that facility was out of bounds to us.

We dockers had been on the ship since 8 a.m. and she was due to sail on high water at 2 p.m. That meant she had to be in the New Lock Entrance by 1.30 p.m. for Thames tugs to tow her out, stern first, through the locks and into the river on the last of the flood tide. As we sat waiting, it was still impossible to see the river at all because the fog continued to cover it, bubbling and steaming like the witches' cauldron in *Macbeth*.

The open foredeck was about 60 feet above the dock water level, but with the flood tide now only five hours away, and the dock water about 12 feet higher than

An Alexander-owned river tug, with its charge, about to enter the locks in one of the upriver docks of the Port of London, 1940s. *(Author's collection)*

the river water level, the ship was still well within the fog layer. We coughed and sneezed, frozen to the very marrow in our bones. We swore at each other, cussed the weather and anything else that took our fancy on the bloody open deck of the SS *Iberia*, a luxury liner that failed to offer us even a minimal bit of shelter from the elements. Pox on the bloody ship, I thought.

At 9.30 everything more than 300 feet from the ship was still obscured by fog. Even the riverside landing stage, from which the *Iberia* should have sailed, was invisible. For safety reasons, she had to remain at her loading berth to embark passengers for their long outward journey to Colombo, Brisbane, Sydney, Melbourne, Adelaide or Perth in Western Australia.

From the ship's foredeck, in the distance one could hear the muffled sounds of the Ovens Buoy off Coalhouse Point, between Gravesend Reach and Lower Hope Point. The mournful sounds of ships' and tugs' sirens came eerily through the fog, too, intermingled with the tooting of ferry boats, which steamed slowly and cautiously back and forth across the river between Tilbury landing stage and Gravesend.

Big Dave was leaning against the ship's rail. He was one of those unfortunate people who have a permanent frown on their face, as though they are carrying all the worries of the world in their head. Anyone who didn't know him might have thought him a funeral director, not a docker. But beneath that stern countenance was a kindly individual – a truly gentle giant of a man with immense physical strength that he must, at times, have had to exercise considerable will-power to contain.

Big Dave was standing next to Alf J. when he suddenly said, 'What's that flashing over there?' He pointed to a spot well above the river about half a mile away. 'Look, there it goes again. It must be some ship in trouble.'

Silence reigned for several minutes as the men gathered at the ship's rails cogitating about the source and meaning of the flashes. Then a guessing game began.

'I think it's the light on the Ovens Buoy. That's got a flashing beam,' said one.

'It can't be that,' said another. 'It's far too high above the water. The Ovens Buoy light is almost level with the river.'

A third gang member ventured to suggest, 'It could be a ship on fire or gone aground. We may be in luck and get picked up for a salvage job tomorrow morning!'

'It may be just a yacht with a faulty riding light that has pulled in close to the shore to get out of the shipping lanes,' said a fourth gang member.

Big Dave turned to Alf and said, 'What do you make of those flashes, Alf?'

'They're naval signals, Dave. I can't grasp exactly what they're signalling, but I'll read it out to you.' He paused to study what, apparently, were a series of Morse code flashes emitted by a ship's Aldis lamp. 'It says something like, "USS Cruiser *Texas*". Then something about the river–something–London–something. I think it said "Lord Mayor". I can't see all the flashes because of this swirling fog.'

Big Dave pulled himself up to his full height of 6 feet 6 inches, stretched his arms, then bent them at the elbows and yawned. He sat down on a bollard and watched for more signalling flashes from the American warship. Alf continued to stand by the ship's rail. The flashes started again, then stopped before beginning once more.

'Is that American cruiser still signalling, Alf? What do you make of it?' said Big Dave.

'I'm a bit rusty at this Morse code now. I've been out of the Royal Navy for ten years, but I shall do my best.'

As the flashes continued, Alf read out, 'To Trinity House pilot station Gravesend, stop. I have anchored my ship in Gravesend Reach, stop. I am still waiting on the arrival of a river pilot, stop. Must make passage to Tower Bridge to arrive not later than 1400 hours, stop. HM the Queen to visit my ship at 1800 hours accompanied by the Lord Mayor of London, stop. Dispatch a river pilot immediately, stop. This signal is from USS *Texas*. End of message, stop.'

'Well,' said Alf. 'Now we know what it is. It's a Yankee warship's captain demanding to be given priority to get up the river to London. He's giving the pilot station a load of toffee about a visit from the Queen. He'll be lucky to get permission from the Port Authority to move his ship in this fog.'

Alf turned round to face the ship's gang with a smirk on his face, winked at them, then sat down on a bollard next to Big Dave.

'I wasn't aware you could read Morse code, Alf,' said Big Dave.

'Why should you have been?'

Seaman E. Roots, a Royal Navy rating
from the 1940s. *(Author's collection)*

'Well, I wasn't to know you were in the navy during the war.'

'I think you mean the Royal Navy, David!'

'That, too,' replied Big Dave.

'Yes, mate. I had a cushy number, too. I was the yeoman of signals on the aircraft carrier *Ark Royal*.'

'Is that a fact? I was always under the impression *Ark Royal* was sunk in the Mediterranean.'

'That is correct. She was.'

'You must have been lucky to have got off her alive when she went down, Alf?'

'Well, in a way I was. When *Ark Royal* was in Alexandria I was rushed ashore with appendicitis. I was in a naval hospital when she left port on her last trip. I lost a lot of good shipmates when she was sent to the bottom of the Mediterranean. I was on several ships that were torpedoed and sunk during the war. I am proud to have served for five years in the Royal Navy. It's a fine service with great traditions.'

'Yes,' Big Dave said, 'I've read about them. Starve 'em, flog 'em, keel haul 'em or hang 'em, wasn't it? Then when they were dead, flog their kit. Great traditions to brag about, I'm sure.'

'That was in the days of sailing ships. You must know the old saying, "wooden ships and iron men"?'

'Yes, so we were told. Now it's "iron ships and wooden men", isn't it?' replied Big Dave. He hoisted his huge body off the bollard and went over to the ship's rail. He watched more spasmodic flashes and called Alf over to witness for himself that the ship was still signalling and that it hadn't moved an inch from its moorings.

'The time must be pressing for them if they want to catch the last of the flood tide,' said Big Dave. 'Do you think the river pilot's got lost in the fog?'

'Of course not. Give them a chance. It will take a pilot cutter some time to get downriver to Lower Gravesend Reach in this poxy weather.'

'How long would you say, Alf?'

'About half an hour.'

While the dockers stood, or sat in small groups about the deck, talking among themselves, Big Dave and Alf leaned against the ship's rail, straining their eyes into the fog for any movement of the American cruiser. Finally, their patience was rewarded.

'The signals have started again, Alf.'

'Yes,' Alf replied. 'I suppose you would like me to decode them for you?'

'If you will be so kind, I would.'

The ship's baggage gang, not wishing to be left out of the fun, crowded along the rail as Alf proceeded to translate the flashes.

A 'block ship' off Arramanches, used in the construction of the Mulberry Harbour, *c.* 1944. *(Author's collection)*

The *Zealandia*, formerly *Empire Winnie*, in Gravesend Reach, 1946. Master: Captain Jim Fryer DSC and Bar. *(Author's collection)*

'Dash dot/dot dash/dot dash dot dot.'

'Cut that out,' Big Dave ordered. 'What does it mean?'

'It simply means "calling".' Alf cupped his hands round his eyes and began. 'Calling Gravesend Trinity House pilot station, stop. Urgently request you send a river pilot immediately, stop. I have previously explained about my urgent appointment in London, stop. This message is from the captain of the USS *Idaho*, stop. Message ends, stop.'

Big Dave's eyebrows knitted together. 'Are there two Yankee ships down there?'

'No,' replied Alf, 'just the one.'

'You told me earlier that ship was called the USS *Texas*.'

'I don't think I did, David,' said Alf as he turned towards the other gang members for confirmation as to the accuracy of his previous statements.

Big Dave glared down at Alf with one eye closed and grunted. 'Right!' he said, and continued to stand by the ship's rail, forever watchful. Alf returned to his seat on a bollard and began to read a *Daily Mirror* he had borrowed from one of the gang.

As Big Dave stood watching, the fog started to fall away slowly, like an ebbing tide. The sun began to grow in circumference as it showed itself above the murk. It looked like a large ball of ice that was slowly turning itself into an orange circle of glowing embers. He then began to see the high landmarks as they emerged slowly through the thinning fog. It was not dissimilar, he thought, to watching objects being revealed on the seashore as the tide recedes. First, ships' masts, then the funnels, bridges and derricks of the vessels closest to the dock entrance came into sight, slowly followed by ships' superstructures as the whole of each vessel began to emerge from the sticky, clinging gauze that had enshrouded them. The tops of dock transit sheds also began to show themselves through the fog blanket. Ships' sirens, which had been wailing mournfully only a few hours beforehand, now took on a melodic note as the fog no longer muffled the shrill warnings from their horns. The rattling of many anchor chains being hauled inboard by capstans heralded the resurrection of Old Father Thames. London's great river was once again coming back to life as vessels of many nations began getting under way to ply their separate routes to every sea port on this earth.

Big Dave was suddenly awakened from his stupor by a sight he had never contemplated. 'Alf!' he called out without turning his head. 'Come over here! I'm sure you will never believe this.'

'What is it?' he asked as he ambled his way over to the ship's rail.

'Your American cruiser is on show, Alf.'

'Oh, where is she now?'

'She's still in the same place as she was before!'

The other members of the baggage gang gathered themselves along the ship's rail to watch. Alf acted as though he had no idea about what was about to unfold.

'What is it, David, old mate?' Alf asked in mock surprise.

'I've just spotted that American naval signaller of yours. He's sending coded signals as fast as he can. He must be on piecework the way his Aldis lamp in flashing away.'

'Really?' said Alf with a smile on his face. 'Where is he?'

'Where you knew he would be all the time, on the top of the Riverside jetty welding a radar mast into place. I'll give you to kid me you was a yeoman of signals in the Royal Navy.' Then, without due ceremony, Big Dave grabbed Alf by the scruff of his neck as if he was a cat about to be put outside the house for the night. He lifted him over the side of the ship so he was dangling some 60 feet above the water in the dock. Then he said, 'You have been extracting the proverbial urine out of David, haven't you, Alfred?'

'Yes, David,' Alf replied. 'I was only joking, but I *was* a yeoman of signals.'

Big Dave breathed out a long, exaggerated sigh and said, 'That would be "retired", of course, and now it could lead to your becoming the late Alfred J.'

He was about to let go of the miscreant when one of the gang shouted out, 'For Christ's sake, Dave, don't drop him. There's a barge down there under the bow.'

Dave hauled Alf back onboard. 'Some people have all the luck, don't they!' he said. Then he promptly turned Alf over and smacked his bottom as one would a naughty small boy. 'That'll teach you not to poke fun at David, you little sod,' he said.

Of course the rest of the gang stood and roared with laughter. Well, wouldn't you have done?

6

BIG DAVE AND THE TUG-OF-WAR TEAM

You have to believe me when I tell you that in the docks in their working clothes, wearing their tattered and torn ex-service uniforms, covered from head to foot in cement or asbestos dust, lamp black or charcoal dust, they were as fearsome looking as they had been when serving their king and country during the battles of the Second World War and the Korean War. Although, had you, reader, seen them in the flesh, you might have mistaken them for a drunken troupe of Black and White Minstrels.

They were, however, eight tall, broad-shouldered men, plus one giant. The eight were all over 6 feet and each weighed not less than 14 stone. There was no surplus fat on any of them: they were all bone and muscle. The ninth, Big Dave, was different, for he was 6 feet 6 inches tall and tipped the scales at 25 stone. He would often joke that when he weighed himself on a set of talking scales they would say to him, 'Don't play about. One of you get off, or one at the time please.'

These men were the dockers tug-of-war team – seven men plus one reserve and Big Dave, who was the team's anchor man.

The Tilbury Dockers' Social Club always entered teams in sporting events on Regatta Day at Gravesend promenade. The tug-of-war team practised anywhere on anything that was considered immovable, pulling with their combined weight and strength in order to achieve unity of purpose, both physically and mentally.

There were also dockers' rowing crews who trained on the river off Gravesend in whalers. Whalers, for the benefit of the uninitiated, are large, heavy, clinker-built rowing boats of the type that were once used for whale hunting in the southern oceans. Whale hunters worked in similar open boats equipped only with oars and rowlocks, harpoons, boat hooks and long lengths of coiled rope that were used in pursuit of harpooned whales.

Although it may be difficult for any reader of this tale to believe, or for that matter to accept, dockers' teams didn't treat training for entry into sporting events in the Gravesend Regatta as a boozing spree. They operated under a strict code of discipline, both the men in the tug-of-war team and the boat crews. They went all out to win once they arrived on the battlefield (or, as sportsmen prefer to call it, 'the sporting arena'), and, as has already been explained, they trained hard.

When the tug-of-war team were in the docks training for Regatta Day, they could often be seen attempting to pull the cast-iron quayside bollards out of the concrete and granite dockside walls. Such training performances would most certainly have engendered in any intrepid stranger the thought that they were watching a party of escaped lunatics, especially as there may have been a ship tied onto the other end of what was, after all, nothing more than a mooring rope or spring.

Another of the implements the tug-of-war team used in training was an old railway shunting engine that rested on a track behind the Port Authority rolling stock repair sheds; the engine was being slowly dismantled by the authority's own railway engineers, who were cannibalizing the parts to repair other engines of the docks' antiquated, clapped-out rolling stock. The tug-of-war team could actually pull that engine along on its track, against its own dead weight, and over the virgin rust that had encrusted the unused railway lines. Believe me, that really did take a combination of weight, great physical strength, brute force and, above all, will-power, qualities the team did not lack. But, as one of their number was heard to remark after a strenuous session under their redoubtable trainer, Eddy L., 'It's a good job they've not taken the steel tyres off that engine yet, isn't it?'

To which another of the team was heard to reply, 'Haven't they? I thought they bloody well had!'

Unfortunately, there seemed to be no other tug-of-war team who trained near the docks against whom they could pit themselves. If there was such a team, they kept firmly to themselves (some people are far more intelligent than one gives them credit for).

Of course, who other than the redoubtable Eddy L. could have been the self-appointed talent-spotter, selector, trainer and manager of such a team. However much anyone might have wished to criticize Eddy's motives or methods, it reluctantly had to be admitted (I have to emphasize the 'reluctantly' bit because the team's success did appear to increase Eddy's head size) he was the best man for the job for three reasons: first, no one else ever offered their services; second, it is doubtful if anyone else in the docks could have done the job; third, and more importantly, he enthused a passion into his men for the skill, the comradeship and the teamwork essential to win matches.

Eddy was always ready to tell 'his' team (and anyone else who would listen) how he had advised Colonel What, What! during his wartime army service that Big Dave was the soldier best suited to take on the wrestling champion of India, and how he had 'guided' and 'trained' Big Dave into becoming the Unofficial Heavyweight Wrestling Champion of the Indian Sub-Continent. But he told them this, he would hasten to explain, in order to get them to understand that, if he could do that with a talentless, oversized lout such as Big Dave, 'who had a brain that could easily be fitted into the eye of a needle', he was sure that, with such obvious athletic material as their goodselves displayed in training, it would beggar him no problem to turn them into tug-of-war champions. Big (good-humoured) Dave usually put a damper on Eddy's denigrating statements with follow-up comments such as, 'That maligning midget carried a bucket of water and a sponge. He didn't even have to use them. If I'd listened to that moronic,

The King of the Belgians public house,
East Street, Gravesend, *c.* 1950.
(Author's collection)

pathetic excuse for a human being to "get stuck into it", that "mobile Buddha" they'd put me into the ring to fight would have killed me. It's no thanks to him I'm still alive.'

'Bodywise you may be, but you're brain dead just the same. It's a pity I didn't let it polish you off,' Eddy would mumble under his breath.

'I heard that!' Big Dave would say, and the team would all laugh.

That was how Eddy had moulded them into a force to be reckoned with. So it is of little wonder, therefore, no one denied Eddy's commitment to the team. However, the methods he used to instil enthusiasm and discipline were those he had learned as a physical training instructor during his service in the army, with a few notable refinements, of course, for he knew from experience how far he could push men, and, more importantly, how far they would be pushed before they began to push back. He also knew that humour played a major role in all training procedures, so he not only joked with the tug-of-war team, but by also making references to their stance, he drilled them into a concerted movement of body, limb and, what he knew was more important, mind. The result of his training endeavours was that the team in action had the appearance of being a single machine. They had been mentally and physically welded into a fighting machine with one simple objective – victory. Eddy had taken every possible known factor into account during the training schedules – except one.

Come Regatta Day, Gravesend promenade was packed with local people and visitors who had come to watch the various events, which were always entertaining. There were, first and foremost, the rowing races into which

The Clarendon Royal Hotel, East Street, Gravesend, facing the River Thames. *(Author's collection)*

publicans from throughout the town entered teams with dubious rowing skills but who were more than capable of holding their own when it came to sinking a pint or two. It should come as no surprise to the reader to learn that the public house teams were invariably less than sober when they arrived on the promenade, and it was quite normal for some of them to fall into the river off the causeway as they tried to scramble into the boats before their race had even got started. After the race many of them were thrown into the river anyway. The winners, when they left the Regatta, hardly ever made it back to the pub they represented, let alone home. Publicans really knew how to look after their rowing crews, although it was a poor oarsman who remembered anything about the events on the following day or even the day after (except for his headache, that is).

The dockers' and stevedores' crews were always competitive. Usually Tilbury dockers rowed against the pulpies (dockers and stevedores who specialized in discharging ships that bought wood pulp from the Scandinavian countries and Canada) or powder monkeys (dockers or stevedores who loaded or discharged ammunition and explosives aboard ships in the lower Thames Estuary). (The downriver anchorages were a precaution in case a ship should explode, the theory being that only the ship, the powder monkeys and the ship's crew would be lost, a minor loss compared with what could be a major catastrophe if a ship's cargo were to explode further upriver nearer an oil installation or a town.)

The dockers and stevedores raced for the coveted King Cup. Their event was always a battle from the start to the finish, especially when the crews got behind the hospital boat that lay just off the causeway that runs into the river off Gravesend promenade and that hid the rowers from the spectators on the river's shore. Then oars would be used like lances to fend off and batter the opposing teams till they turned round the buoy down the river below the hospital boat and were on the home straight. The crews would then sedately swing their craft into the home stretch of water and pull like hell for the finishing line. Butter? Well, it wouldn't melt in their mouths now, would it?

To enhance the sporting events there was always a funfair that played its own music. The music was never so loud that it drowned one's speech or impaired one's hearing. Nor did it overwhelm the cries, cheers and jeers of the crowds as they egged on competitors in the various events that were taking place along the whole length of the promenade. There was a greasy pole, for instance. It was about 20 feet high from the ground to the top, greased along the whole of its length. It was great fun watching all sorts of characters, some drunk and others sober, trying all sorts of tricks to climb that slimy, wretched pole, but it was not a stunt to try oneself. There were also the egg and spoon race, the sack race, the over-60s race, the under-10s race, the ladies' race (although no one would call a few of them ladies if their language was anything to go by). You give a name to a race and there are always competitors available to take part in it. It was all good, harmless fun, till someone accused someone else of cheating, then a glorious punch-up would ensue, enjoyed by all the spectators.

Regatta days are still always great fun for the locals and their children, but it is also true to say they are financially lucrative for the soft drinks, hot dogs and ice-cream vendors. They make a packet of money, as does the licensed publican who is lucky enough to get the sole rights to sell beer and spirits all day and up till midnight in a large marquee set aside specially for the purpose. The marquee is provided and installed by the brewery company whose publican has obtained the licence for the particular event.

The publican chosen to run a bar at the town regatta that is the setting for this tale was none other than Little Fred, Big Dave's friend and bosom pal of yesteryear, that little prankster, who always managed to get Big Dave into some form of trouble with his off-beat antics. Oddly enough – and this fact cannot be emphasized too strongly, especially to exponents of the game – the beer marquee had been erected very close to the bunting-draped, roped-off tug-of-war arena. One of the main guy ropes of the marquee was attached to a heavy steel peg that had been driven into the ground some 20 feet away from the tent's open end. Little Fred was serving at his bar, collecting empty glasses and refereeing at some of the events. This meant he could go walk-about to collect empty glasses when the bar was running short (and get up to mischief, as was his forte).

As the day wore on and the evening began to draw in, the twilight caused the setting sun to turn into a bright-red ball of fire as it prepared itself for bed, and the lights of the fairground area began to come on, causing ripples to reflect from the water of the river's surface. Music from the funfair began to get louder. The stage was set for the tug-of-war teams to get down to business, which they did.

The riverside entrance to the Old Falcon Hotel, East Street, Gravesend, 1920s. It was the haunt of Bawley Bay shrimp fishermen, Thames barge skippers, watermen and lightermen, and merchant seamen returning home after a long voyage. *(Author's collection)*

There were four trained tug-of-war teams and four made up of half-drunk hobbledehoys, wretched, pimply-faced youths who had been coerced by fellows of their own ilk to 'go forward and try your luck' against teams, one of which, they were told, was made up of County Police officers. This was a challenge they just could not resist. The preliminary matches were soon dispensed with as the County Police pulled the pimply-faced hobbledehoys into a pile, and dockers' teams quickly put an end to any thoughts other Jack the Lads had of getting further than the first round. Of course those matches were a laugh in themselves, as the lads, with arms and legs sticking out in all directions, pulled, snatched and yanked at the rope but could not budge the trained teams one inch. When it was obvious the lads were on the point of collapse from their pathetic exertions, the trained opposing team's coach gave the order, 'Pull-one, pull-two, pull-three!'

Then the white rope marker, together with the inebriated social misfits, some on their feet, others on their backs, came over the line as easily as a cork being extracted from a wine bottle by a professional waiter. Some little time was allowed to elapse for the cheers, jeers, tears and general mayhem to die down. Then came the main event, the final between the County Police and the dockers.

Now I have to admit I may have misled the reader with regard to the constituents of the dockers' team, for I omitted to say that in the preliminary rounds it consisted of seven of the full team and the reserve – and this does have a bearing on the tale.

The referee for the tug-of-war final was to be none other than Little Fred.

'I'm tossing a coin,' he said. 'The winner takes the marquee end, the loser takes the canal end. Is that understood?' He asked the police team captain to call.

'Heads,' he said.

Then without showing either of the team captains the coin, Little Fred simply said, 'Heads it is. Police to the marquee end; dockers to the canal end.'

The two teams began to line up, with one exception; the dockers' reserve team member walked away into the beer tent – and Big Dave strode out. He walked to the end of the line, took turns of the rope over his shoulder and round his waist, and stood there like the Colossus of Rhodes. Not a sound came from the crowd: they were too numbed with surprise. The police team, too, stood with folded arms, looking at this giant. They were all County Police officers and equal in size and weight to the other members of the dockers' team, but the dockers' secret weapon was a bit more than they had expected.

Big Dave stood his ground, the normal deadpan expression on his face. Little Fred gave the order to take the strain. Both teams laid back, testing the weight and strength of their opponents, neither gaining an inch on the other. Big Dave stood holding the rope with one hand and scratching his head with the other.

The back entrance from the River Thames to the New Falcon, West Street, Gravesend, 1950s. *(Author's collection)*

The Beehive public house in West Street, Gravesend. All the public houses in this area of Gravesend were frequented by merchant seamen, barge skippers, watermen and lightermen, dockers and stevedores. *(Author's collection)*

Then the police team made its move.

'Pull-one,' their coach called.

Nothing happened. Half a minute passed as slowly as half an hour.

The police coach tried again. 'Pull-one,' he repeated.

Again nothing happened, the police laid back on the rope to wait for the order for another try, but Eddy didn't give them a chance.

'Pull-one,' he ordered. The dockers stamped their left feet into the soft turf in unison, moving backwards as if they were one man with a long shadow. The marquee behind the police team began to shake.

'Pull-one-two,' Eddy called again. The marquee shook again, but the police held their ground, although they were close to going over the line.

'Again!' roared Eddy. 'Pull-one-two-three-four-five-six-seven.' As the dockers moved back, with Big Dave straining the rope with all his great strength, the police team came forward, bracing themselves with every sinew, their feet skimming over the evening-dew-covered grass . . . and the marquee behind them began to follow, collapsing in a heap. Yells and screams emanated from within, mostly from customers who were spilling their beer. The police and dockers ran to help those who were trapped. Unbelievably, no one was hurt – this was probably because most of them were too drunk to care. Then questions began to be asked as to why the marquee had collapsed. Big Dave became suspicious; he walked to the police end of the marquee and looked down at the steel peg holding up the main guy line. Little Fred was standing beside him with a blank, but not surprised, expression on his face. Big Dave grabbed him by the scruff of the neck.

'What's that?' he said.

'Good God, David,' said Little Fred. 'It looks as if the tug rope got itself tangled round the guy rope's support peg.'

'Yes, it does,' said Big Dave, 'and it also miraculously made itself fast with a double half-hitch and finished up with a lighterman's knot just to make sure it wouldn't slip off the end of the main support peg. Clever ropes they make these days to hold marquees in position.'

'Well, yes it is,' replied Little Fred sheepishly. 'Although I distinctly remember you telling me about a bloke in India who could climb up a rope – the Indian rope trick? I'm sure it was you who told me that.'

'Now cut that old toffee out and own up like the man you would like to have been, if you had ever grown up,' said Big Dave. 'What have you been up to, tiny man?'

'Well, David, you know how it is. I had a wager the police would win the tug-of-war match. I thought you lot would get tired pulling against the police team,

The Ship & Lobster public house, The Sea Wall, Denton, Gravesend. Thames sailing barges, in times past, laid off the Ship & Lobster to ride out rough weather and fogs. River police used a shed at the back of the premises as a mortuary. The pub was also used for smuggling. *(Author's collection)*

more especially if they had a little bit of help from a friend,' said Little Fred. 'Anyway, I was going to treat all of you to a nice long drink on my winnings. How was I to know you lot would wreck my marquee?'

'Well, I must admit you didn't know that, but no, we wouldn't dream of letting you buy us a drink now you have lost your bet. We'll get you one, instead.'

With that Big Dave picked Little Fred up above his head, walked over to the riverside where the tide was just beginning to ebb, and threw the miscreant out into the river, where he landed with a splash and disappeared under the water. Everyone who could get close to the riverside let out a loud cheer as Little Fred came to the surface.

'Help! Help!' he yelled out. 'I can't swim.'

Big Dave was not in a forgiving mood. 'Don't worry,' he called back, 'neither can I, but the tide's on the ebb. You should be able to touch the bottom in half an hour.'

THE FINALE

The police team accepted that the dockers had won the tug-of-war match. One of them dived in the river and pulled Little Fred out of the water (but not before he had ducked him a few times on his way back to the shore). It was a fitting end to a really enjoyable day at the Gravesend Regatta, although Big Dave couldn't understand why Little Fred didn't think so. It may have been because the two teams carried him back to his marquee and made him call drinks on the house.

The collapse of the marquee was put down to a freak wind getting under the canopy and lifting the steel peg holding up the mainstay. This must have been Little Fred's account of what caused the marquee's collapse, simply because it read more like a description of a Thames barge's mast being lowered. Trust him, the little sod.

7

DOC AND THE SUGAR BOAT INCIDENT

Doc was a 'green horn' – that is, he had only this very day entered the port transport industry, and through his ignorance he did something that would be unthinkable to established registered dock workers: he voluntarily gave his attendance book to a ship worker, who was in charge of a ship berthed alongside Tilbury Riverside cargo jetty that was due to load sugar.

'The man must be deranged. He's obviously escaped from a lunatic asylum,' one of the lads was jokingly heard to remark. 'Are you sure he's safe to work with?'

'Well, he looks harmless enough – for an idiot, that is,' said another.

No docker or stevedore in his right mind would volunteer to work on loading or discharging ships carrying sugar in the enclosed docks, let alone on Tilbury Riverside cargo jetty. When ship workers had picked up their regular gangs in the Dock Labour Board compound, and a sugar boat was berthed somewhere in the docks, it was simply a matter of time before the men waiting on the free call heard the Tannoy system in the compound announce 'All books in'; it was then a short wait to see which of them had drawn the short straw and been called to work on the sugar boats. It was, without doubt, like playing a game of Russian roulette with one's livelihood. The reason for their reluctance to work on sugar loading or discharging operations was not that it was hard graft – there were very few jobs in the docks that were not sweated labour. It was simply because the piecework rate was so low it was a hard slog for a very small pay reward.

Bagged imported sugar usually came in 3-hundredweight hessian sacks. The sacks were sometimes stuck together in slabs, like big bars of sticky toffee, and pom-pom guns had to be used to separate them before they could be discharged into lighters or barges.

Refined export sugar, on the other hand, was invariably exported in 2-hundredweight hessian sacks. The piecework rate for this export commodity was 2s 11d per ton, shared between twelve men – in other words, less than 3d per ton to each man.

Sugar for export was brought downriver in barges or lighters, direct from the Tate & Lyle refinery in Silver Town, north Woolwich. Tate & Lyle is a major refiner and wholesale supplier of sugar. The term sugar is generic and covers a

Millwall Dock, 1955. *(Illustrated London News, 1955)*

group of carbohydrates, including sucrose, glucose, fructose and maltose. To put it in plain, ordinary, simple language, to you and me sugar generally means sucrose, a substance that is obtained from sugar beet, sugar cane or sugar maple.

When the job of loading a ship was ready to start, the refined sugar was made up by the men working in lighters or barges (the bargehands) into twelve-sack sets. The sets of sugar were hoisted aboard the ship by cranes or winches. When ships arrived in port, they were worked ten hours a day when loading or discharging, or for a 'short night' (that is, from 8 a.m. till midnight) or an 'all night' (that is, from 8 a.m. one day till 8 a.m. the next), if the vessel was a liner, due to sail on a schedule and required to depart at a certain time. As far as sugar jobs were concerned, the overtime rate on piecework was paid at just above the day rate between 5 to 7 p.m. This meant there was very little financial incentive for men to work overtime on sugar loading or discharging ships, other than to get back into the Dock Labour Board compound in the hope of getting a more financially rewarding job.

On some occasions, employers invoked the 'you shall work overtime if required to do so' rule, a rule contained in post-war working agreements that had been drawn up between the port employers and officials of trade unions representing registered dock workers – the unions agreed without consulting the membership on this issue. The rule was contained in a clause introduced into dock working practices and conditions during the Second World War. It had been put in place, together with a continuity rule, in order to get ships discharged or loaded more quickly and made ready for protection by the Royal Navy when they joined a convoy. But when used in peacetime, it was a flagrant abuse of the liberty of man and totally disregarded dock workers' rights to choose whether they wished to work overtime (more especially after having been press-ganged into the job in the first instance). It was heavy-handed impertinence on the employers' part, an abuse of employment power that caused a great deal of resentment and bad blood between ship owners, managers and dock workers, especially as the remedy to the problem lay in the ship owners' hands.

However, this is not to say that some ship's gangs did not earn reasonable wages discharging sugar. Regular stevedore and docker gangs, working afloat off the Woolwich buoys, discharged several hundred tons of sugar each day between 8 a.m. and 5 p.m., working over-side under a ship's derricks. In addition, thousands of tons of sugar were discharged with the use of grab-cranes at Samuel Williams's riverside wharf at Dagenham docks, Essex. The 'down-holders' had to clear loose sugar from behind stringer boards with shovels, an operation any docker would have called 'a doodle of a job' – stringer boards are wooden boards attached to a ship's ribs to protect the steel plates from cargo damage.

When hessian-bagged sugar was loaded aboard vessels moored to Tilbury Riverside cargo jetty, barges and lighters were brought inside, between the jetty and the shore, occupying the relatively calm water on the land side of the cargo jetty while they were being discharged. The shoreline protruded into the river behind and below the New Lock Entrance. The tidal river water was, therefore, kept away from the immediate areas between the Riverside cargo jetty and the rock-faced sea wall, and this created a tranquil, smooth, shallow basin where barges were worked without the bargehands becoming seasick, as they would if they were working in barges secured to a ship on the river side of the jetty, which was constantly being buffeted by waves made by a fast-running tide and the bow-waves of ships making way up or down the river.

The method of loading ships from barges moored inside Tilbury cargo jetty entailed using two cranes attached to the jetty. The shoreside crane lifted sets of sugar from the barge onto the top of the cargo jetty. The riverside crane took the sets off the jetty to be lowered into a ship's hold, where a stowage gang would then back the sugar (that is, carry the 2-hundredweight sacks on their backs) to the allotted stowage. On the occasion of this tale, the sugar was being stowed in number 2 upper 'tween deck, at the after end of the hatch. The ship's gang, except Doc, had been allocated to the vessel from the Dock Labour Board compound. Doc was the odd man out, having been picked up on the free call that very day.

Doc was very quietly spoken, a likeable, inoffensive chap, who had no idea what he was letting himself in for when he became a docker. He was quickly given the nickname Doc when it had become known to his fellow dockers that he had been a nurse and had worked at the local hospital.

'Bloody psychiatric nurse,' one man mumbled. 'He must have been to volunteer for a soddin' job like this. If you get dealing with a load of nutters for a long time it's odds on you'll wind up like them.'

'Yes,' said his mate. 'Is that your excuse, too?'

'It isn't bloody funny, you fool. That loony business could be contagious.'

All the down-holders in the ship's gang turned and looked at him, then burst out laughing.

'It takes a bloody idiot to know one,' the down-hold foreman said. 'Come on, that's enough of that nonsense. Let's get on with this job.'

Doc's father-in-law also worked in the docks, and he was employed as an after-foreman for a stevedoring labour contractor that serviced P&O liners of the Far East and Australasian fleet. No doubt Dad had the intention of securing Doc a job with him as soon as an opportunity presented itself. (Nepotism was one of the endemic scourges of the port transport industry.) It was Dad who had advised Doc to give his attendance book to a ship worker. But he had not been in the Dock Labour Board compound to tell him who he should not 'shape up for'. Consequently, poor Doc had got himself lumbered as a down-holder on this ship, a loading sugar boat, manned by a gang of pressed men. His only consolation was that he had not been picked to be a bargehand. That was a much more physically demanding job that would, as like as not, have finished him as a docker.

Doc was tall, with light-brown hair and bright blue-eyes. He was pale of face and thin in body. He had less muscle on his arms and legs than could be found on a sea mollusc, a creature with a similar-sounding name. He wore thick, steel-rimmed glasses. He had a curious gait insofar as his slim shoulders stayed rigid while his knees appeared to be semi-stiff and jerky. It was as though he had had a partially successful fusing operation on both of his hips and knees. This may have been the reason for what was to happen to him shortly.

The first set of sugar that came down the hold was lowered to the deck and made fast with two chocks of dunnage and a sisal rope, which was then lashed to a steel stanchion. The stanchion was welded to the deck floor and ceiling to support the ship's upper deck when she was carrying deck cargo. The first set of sugar was used as a base for a table on which a cargo running board was placed, and when future sets came down the hold, they were landed on the running board, at the back of which the gang had laid two sacks of sugar. When the bottom sacks at the back of the following sets landed on the two bags of sugar, the set was tipped over, leaving all the sacks standing upright. The down-holders formed a line, then one by one they carried the bags on their backs to the stowage, where the down-hold foreman and his mate stowed them.

Now, I must explain that gangs working over the jetty were made up of two crane drivers, one top hand, a down-hold foreman, a change-over man (who worked on the jetty and took the rope off one crane hook and placed it on the second crane hook), four bargehands and five down-holders. (One crane driver and the change-over man were paid pro rata to the gang's piecework earnings.)

The second set having been landed on the running board, the physical hard work of stowing the sugar cargo began. Most of the backers (the men carrying the sacks) had managed to get pieces of canvas or old paper cement bags to put over their shoulders to stop the sugar chafing the skin off their backs and drawing blood. The dockers formed themselves into a line, and as his turn came, each one took hold of the ears of a bag and carried it to the stowage. Doc was the last in the line, having held back so he could see what the procedure was. He picked up his first 2-hundredweight sack of sugar and staggered forward across the deck to the stowage. His second effort saw him buckling at the knees. With his third bag, he stumbled a few yards, his knees gave way under him and he fell, face down on the 'tween deck hatches with the 2-hundred weight sack of sugar pinning him to the deck. Unfortunately, it looked quite funny, seeing him spread out, lying down there, looking like a huge tortoise whose shell was too heavy for it to carry about.

The dockers went on working, walking round him to get to the stowage. One jokingly said, 'I hope that lazy sod's not on the tick note. He's bloody asleep on the job already and we've only just started work.'

Another one said, 'By the way he's lying there, do you think he's bedridden?' To which someone replied, 'It looks more like sack-ridden, to me.'

The gang continued to clear the sets of sugar as poor Doc lay prostrate, halfway between the landing table and the stowage. None of the gang spoke to him as they continued to carry the sacks of sugar to the stowage. It was some time before the barge bay was cleared and they removed the offending bag from his back. The down-hold foreman called up to the top hand and told him he was swapping Doc with the change-over man on the jetty. Doc objected bitterly, saying he would master the job if it should kill him, which it would have done. However, there was a compromise. Doc swapped places with one of the loaders on the landing table. He saw the job out to its conclusion and it was just as well for him that he did: the Docklands were no place to lose face.

Tomlins Terrace, Limehouse, July 1960. *(Tower Hamlets Local History Library)*

In Conclusion

In the mid–1950s, the trade unions negotiated a rise in the piecework rate with the port employers for loading and discharging bagged sugar. It rose to 3*d* per ton. The tabloids carried a story that went something like this: 'Dockers demand an increase in the price paid for discharging sugar. Sugar prices are set to rise by a penny per pound.'

Dockers and stevedores were awarded an extra 3*d* a ton for their labour to share between twelve men; the sugar processors got an extra 237*d* per ton. The media never did publish that piece of news. Well, they wouldn't would they? Not to exonerate those 'bloody dockers'.

8

A BEAUTIFUL PASSENGER

The Orient liner SS *Orion* was returning from its voyage to Australia. It was in the New Lock Entrance, Tilbury Docks. The ship's captain and pilot were waiting for the lock to fill and the inner lock gates to open so that Port Authority steam tugs moored close to the dock side of the inner lock could cast off to assist the Thames river tugs, which had towed the ship into the lock from the river, to take her to her allotted berth.

Baggage gangs had been picked up in the Dock Labour Board compound on the 7.30. a.m. free call to attend on the ship's passengers, and they were standing by, ready with wheelbarrows, to carry passengers' personal effects to their private cars or taxi cabs. (Those vehicles were parked in the space between two transit sheds.)

A railway engine, with eight carriages, was on the track at the rear of the transit sheds, slowly hissing steam. It was waiting to take third-class passengers to Fenchurch Street station in the City of London, from where they would have to make their own way to their final destinations.

Low tables, constructed from cargo running boards set on trestles (trestles that would soon be used for discharging the ship's frozen meat cargo), had been put up in a cargo shed. On them, customs officers would examine the contents of passengers' suitcases and any other such paraphernalia – packages that had either been carried ashore by cabin stewards, or put ashore from the main deck in cargo nets by quay cranes or with the ship's own derricks. The effects would be placed in rows close to the customs examination tables; passengers would have to find their own baggage and then present all of the items to a customs officer.

It was the practice of customs officers to appear on the scene, at their benches, shortly before the first-class passengers began to disembark. I was always of the opinion that the reason for this policy was that it meant the customs officers would not have to demean themselves by rubbing shoulders with those of us who were overtly considered to be socially and intellectually *personae non gratae* in their eyes during those class-conscious days. We of the common herd, that is.

As the water in the lock drew level with that in the dock, the lock gates slowly swung wide open. Tug crews unhooked the ropes securing their vessels to the quayside bollards and steamed astern to take up pre-allotted positions from which to draw the huge ship from the lock to her berth. Ropes, with Turks' heads woven

A Royal Mail ship of the Orient Steam Ship Company entering the New Lock Entrance to Tilbury Docks, 1950s. *(Author's collection)*

into them, were thrown from the liner onto the tugs' sterns. The tugs' deck crews hauled them in and attached the wire hawsers which the ropes held onto the tugs' towing hooks. Signals were given by hoots from the liner's siren. The tugs slowly drew the vessel from the lock into the dock and onto her discharging berth. As the last of the mooring ropes and wires was secured onto the quayside bollards, I climbed up the three 20-foot vertical steel ladders into the Stothert & Pitt crane cabin and swung the jib over a gangway that was lying ready.

It was now the turn of the shore gang slingers to attach pre-prepared wires to the crane's hook so I could raise the gangway and slew it into the forward saloon door, where it was made fast by the ship's crew, specifically for first-class-passenger priority disembarkation. The ship's gang began the task of discharging the passengers' cabin baggage, which had been brought into the forward foyer by the cabin stewards.

Once the gangway was placed in the foyer door, the hatch cover was raised and my job was concluded till the ship's gang began to uncover the deck hatches and to discharge cargo. I descended from the cabin, down the ladders to the quay and stood by a safety barrier, close to the gangway. I was talking to an Orient Line security watchman when the first passenger came out through the saloon door and began her walk down the gangway. Well, it wasn't just an ordinary walk. It was more like that of a highly trained model, exhibiting those fancy, totally useless frocks (the rag trade prefer to call them dresses because it sounds posh) to be sold at exorbitant prices to women with more money than they know what to do with.

She came out of the starboard saloon door of the ship, this beautiful creature, and slowly traipsed her way down the gangway. She was swinging her slim hips from side to side as though she was traversing a catwalk, tilting her head slightly upwards as though trying to avert her gaze from the common herd, but being well aware every eye within sight of her was watching. The men of the baggage gangs stood, leaning on the shafts of their wheelbarrows, staring; taxi drivers standing by the safety barriers were staring; second- and third-class passengers, waiting on the after decks to disembark, were staring. She was a sight to behold.

She descended the gangway with one hand on the safety rail, holding the other hand at shoulder height in a swan-neck position. She was tall and slim and had the facial features of the *Venus de Milo*. She was wearing a red summer dress, with a flower design in bright colours, which finished just below her knees. She had white silk stockings, the old-fashioned style with broad seams that ran down the back of her long legs. Her peep-toe shoes were red. Her wide-brimmed summer hat was white. It enhanced the colour of her dress, giving it a 3D effect while at the same time highlighting her facial features, which in turn were further enhanced by the elbow-length white gloves she wore. She had a white leather handbag that hung down from her shoulder to slightly above her right hip. She was wearing very little make-up, only a smattering of lipstick, the same red as her dress. Her perfume had a mildly exotic smell and it wafted after her like a misty shadow. She was, and knew she was, a beautiful woman.

As she came level with me on the quay she asked in a rasping voice, 'Where's the khars spark'd, cobber?'

'The what?' I said, absolutely dumbfounded by a voice that could not possibly have come from this beautiful woman.

'Are you deaf or just bloody stupid, blue?' she said with an obvious, deep Australian drawl.

I was just about to ask her if she could speak in English, but instead I decided to humour her so I simply replied, 'A bit of both, I think?'

She stepped towards me menacingly, then she smiled through a set of teeth that shone like pearls, put her lips close to my ear and shouted, 'I'm sorry, mate, I wasn't aware of your affliction.' Then, as loud as she could, she yelled into my ear, 'Where's the bloody khars spark'd?'

I put my finger in my ear to clear it and shook my head. 'Madam,' I said, 'I don't know what you are talking about. I don't know what a bloody khars spark'd is!'

'It's a spark where they keep khars.'

'Oh, you mean a car park?'

'Christ Almighty,' she said in a lower tone of voice that I wasn't meant to hear, 'don't tell me they've got another Pommie bloody Professor Higgins-type Eliza Doolittle elocution teacher here?'

Not wishing to pursue the khars spark'd debate any further (the illusion of this vision already having destroyed itself before my eyes), I pointed between the two transit sheds.

'That's where the car park is,' I said. 'But before you go to the car park, you will have to clear HM Customs first. That means let them examine what's in your baggage.'

I led her to the transit shed door and pointed to the long lines of suitcases, travelling trunks and other packages, and the low-level benches, behind which stood the customs officers. I explained to her that she had to get a porter, ask him to find her cases and take them to be seen by one of the customs officers. She bent down and kissed my cheek, patted me on the head as if I were her small son being sent off to school, gave me an Australian sixpence from her purse and yelled in my ear again.

'I'm sorry about your affliction. It must be a big 'andicap to you, blue,' and she just seemed to drift away slowly into the transit shed. Then she was gone.

'Well, well, well!' said the Orient Line security watchman. 'She must be one of the most beautiful women in the world.'

'Yes!' I replied. 'It's a great pity she has to open her mouth.'

9

A CHEAP LUNCH

There had been very little work about for some weeks and we had been dabbing on at the Dock Labour Board office. 'Dabbing on' was the term used by dockers and stevedores to denote that a green stamp had been used to prove their attendance on the free call on any particular day. Another term used was 'bomping on'. There is no such word in the dictionary, but it all came down to the same thing – there was no work available within any of the docks in the Port of London or an adjacent port, and the surplus labour had been sent home on the fall-back guarantee of one 'turn'. (It would be one of the eleven turns that made up a working week – two for each day from Monday to Friday and a single one for Saturday.)

Now, the lads I worked with, when we could get a job, were all young men in their early twenties. They had not long completed their period of national service (giving up two or three years of their young lives for king or queen and the protection of the realm on shirt-button wages). Some of us were trying to earn

Transit shed, London Dock. (PLA Monthly, *October 1952*)

and save some money to get married. That wasn't possible without stringent economies. Eric (Bonar Calleano's double) and I devised a simple scheme of our own – a 'pure-theory' economic approach to retaining earned income, you understand, that was based on saving by reducing our financial outlay.

We had managed, Eric and I, to get into a regular ship's gang, loading stores for the British Army of the Rhine on General Steam Navigation short sea traders, which were a subsidiary part of the P&O Line. They operated from number 5 transit shed, Tilbury Docks. It was a regular run for the boats that arrived on Tuesday afternoon with a part-cargo of returned military stores. These were quickly discharged so that the boats could be made ready for loading first thing on Wednesday morning.

Being short sea traders, they took only two days to load, but army stores were mostly paid for by the measurement ton for piecework purposes. Therefore, the ship's loading gangs could earn well for their two and a half days of employment, and working Tuesday afternoon, Wednesday and Thursday meant that we had covered five of the eleven compulsory dabbing turns in a week and had six dabbing periods to sign on at the Dock Labour Board office to qualify for the dabbing concessions – that is full back money, payable for the non-employed periods when we had reported for work. It was, therefore, essential to us that we minimize our outlay and maximize the value of our wages by cutting back on any non-essential item and finding an alternative outlet to which we could transfer costs.

Now, as this tale is about food, it has to be stressed here that the Port of London Authority provided subsidized meals in a large canteen. The building that now housed the canteen had been built to accommodate black-leg labour, that is non-union men who had been smuggled into the docks in covered barges to break the strikes of 1911 and 1912. The Port Authority, at the time of this tale, charged 2s 6d for a dinner, sweet and a mug of tea.

Eric and I, however, thought we could do better than that on price. Our plan was to filch some tins of food from the ship's cargo and smuggle them into the Port Authority gear and store shed. We would then proceed to the fish and chip shop outside the dock, and buy a fourpenny bag of chips each before making a hasty return to the gear and store shed (before the chips got cold) where the storekeeper subsidized his wages at lunchtime by selling tea at 2d a mug. By buying chips at fourpence and a mug of tea at twopence, we would be saving 2s a day. Nobody could argue with the theory from a basic economics point of view. However, the application in practice was a bit iffy as it turned out.

We carried out the first part of our plan in good order when our ship's gang stopped work to go for lunch. We then purloined and smuggled some tins of food off the ship and into the Port Authority gear and store shed. We hadn't had time to read what the contents of the tins were, but as they were tins of food, processed by a well-known manufacturer and destined for the British Army, we simply took it as read that it was a quality product. In fact it turned out to be apple purée with custard, specially produced for babies.

'Never mind,' said Eric, 'it's sure to be wholesome. Let's get the chips, and sod the cost, get a twopenny crusty roll each as well.'

We dashed out to the fish and chip shop, past the police gate where the Port Authority police constable eyed us with deep suspicion. We purchased our chips and got some free crackling, too. Then we slipped into the baker's and bought two crusty bread rolls before making our way quickly back to the gear and store shed.

We each pierced our tins of apple purée and custard and put them on top of the combustion stove to heat up. We quickly devoured our chips and roll. We borrowed a spoon each from the gearer and storekeeper, who sat fascinated at our antics. We scoffed down the purée and custard. We sat licking our lips, totally satisfied with our efforts. After all, we had saved 1s 10d each. Not bad, we thought.

The storekeeper said, 'You two are obviously not married? You've got no children, have you?' We both shook our heads.

'Pretty athletic are you?' We both nodded and said yes.

'You had better be,' he said. 'They don't issue nappies with those tins of baby food,' and he laughed and laughed – so did his mates.

Eric and I got up to make our way back to work. The gearer, storekeeper and their mates were still roaring with laughter as we left.

'Do you think they were trying to tell us something?' I asked Eric.

'No! It was a bit of jealousy on their part. After all, they only had sandwiches. Did you notice how they toasted them on that combustion stove? They must have tasted bloody awful, what with those coke fumes getting into the bread. Now, my old mate, we, on the other hand, had chips and crackling with a crusty bread roll, followed by apple purée and custard, washed down with a pint mug of tea. Not bad for the price at 8d each, I say.'

'No,' I agreed.

We got back to the ship and were down the hold, about to start work on the first set of cargo, when Eric made a dash for the ladder. I know he had been in the Royal Navy, but he took off up that ladder faster than a fireman can descend his pole when called out to attend to a blaze. He dashed off down the gangway and was soon out of sight. The top hand called down, 'What's wrong with him?' just as I rushed past like a bat out of hell in the general direction that Eric had taken.

I caught up with Eric just as he got to the communal toilet, some 400 yards from the ship. No words were spoken as we dashed in as fast as we could to relieve ourselves. 'Bloody hell,' he called over the separating partition. 'That was close to an embarrassing catastrophe. What do you think caused it?'

'Try thinking about what the gearer and storekeeper said: "they don't issue nappies with those tins of baby food". He didn't even mention soggy chips and crackling with vinegar. Him and his mates could have warned us, but they chose to have a good old laugh at our expense. Don't worry, I know where there are some bales of senna pods. We will have the last laugh, and it will be on them. Just you wait and see. We'll see just how athletic they are.'

We did, and they couldn't run anywhere near as fast as us. They became known as the baggy-trousered, geriatric, cross-quays runners.

10

THE SHIP THAT NEVER LOVED ME

She was a beautiful ship, the P&O liner SS *Himalaya*. She had the silhouette of a sea goddess, if the construction of ships could be placed in such a category. She was, as a matter of fact, one of the Pacific & Orient Shipping Company's 'Queens of the Oceans', for it had several ships similar to her. Yes, she was beautiful, and what is more, yes, I am sure she was aware of her beauty, just as I am aware of the beauty of the marble statue, the *Venus de Milo*, and of the late Hollywood film actresses Marilyn Monroe and Ava Gardner.

The SS *Himalaya* wasn't a big ship by the standards of her day. She had a gross displacement of some 28,000 tons or thereabouts. But unfortunately for me, she was the ship that never loved me. I do suppose she had a good reason to dislike me, and I'm sure she really did bear me a grudge.

She had fine, elegant lines, with her buff-cream funnel and white-painted hull. As a queen, she expected to be paid homage, not to be disfigured, which was the crime I committed against her. This happened when she came into Tilbury Docks to discharge her cargo before going into dry dock to have her keel scrubbed and repainted, her boiler tubes replaced, her cabins, ballroom and dining saloons revamped, revarnished and recarpeted, and maintenance work carried out on her engines. She was to be titivated, like a woman about to go out on a special date, before she was ready to return to her royal domain, the Seven Seas.

She had recently returned to the Port of London from a Far East voyage, and had at first berthed at Tilbury Riverside landing stage, where she disgorged her passengers and their personal effects before entering the enclosed docks proper. The ship's discharging gangs had been picked up in the Dock Labour Board compound, and were then told off to their places of work on the ship. The down-holders made their way to the various hatches, the top hands and winch drivers went up to the open deck, and the crane drivers climbed up into the crane cabins. Then the task of discharging the ship's cargo began in earnest.

I had been detailed by Charlie S., the ship worker, to drive the crane at number 5 hatch. It was an 80-foot jibbed, 3-ton lifting capacity, electric Stothert & Pitt quay crane. Number 5 hatch was at the stern and the hatch cover was a large steel lid that was raised on hinges and bolted against a bulkhead behind the cargo working space and the ship's electric winches. Protruding over the ship's side

Ships berthed at London Dock. *(Tower Hamlets Local History Library)*

were davits that each held two lifeboats, a small one inside a larger one. Above and towards the stern was a 30-foot flagpole that flew the commodore's flag when he was aboard. It also had an electric riding light attached to the top.

Although I was operating an 80-foot crane, the cabin only came just above the ship's safety rail, and the davits holding the ship's lifeboats were above the cabin roof. A hoisted set of cargo only just cleared the ship's upper housing by a few feet. But, as the vessel rose out of the water with the discharge of her cargo, those feet became inches. The only way to take cargo ashore by crane was to hoist the set up to the crane's upper limit above the ship's hatch, luff the jib in towards the crane cabin, while, at the same time, swinging the set aft between the davits and the flagpole. Then it was necessary to swing the crane's jib aft and luff it, bringing the set behind the flagpole before slewing it round the ship's stern, clear of the lifeboats, and out over the transit shed. Then I had to luff in to bring the set onto the pitch between the crane tracks, where the quay gang was waiting to move it into the transit shed.

Now I'm sure I don't have to remind the reader that dockers and stevedores were pieceworkers, and every second counted in our endeavours to maximize our wages. The crux of the problem, in this particular case, was the flagpole. I knew that if it was taken down, I would be able to lift sets out of the hold, slew them round the ship's stern behind the davits, out over the transit shed, luff in on the jib, and land them on the pitch in one simple operation. I sent a message to the ship's mate requesting him to take the obstruction down and make my job a lot easier and a lot safer for those people working under the crane. After an interminable time he condescended to come up on deck, give a cursory inspection and make a determination relating to the problem.

Of course, being a P&O company officer, he had to do this with great ceremony and panache. The mate turned up with an entourage befitting the queen of England, let alone a queen of the oceans, to survey the area and decide the best way *he* thought the problem could be dealt with, if at all. He finally ruled that it was not a feasible proposition to get the ship's electrician to unplug the electric socket at the base of the flagpole and the Lascar crew to lift the flagpole out of its holding brackets. He stood by with his underlings, watching me juggling with the crane to get a few sets ashore. Then, while I was landing a set of cargo on the quay and out of his sight, he and his consorts disappeared.

Now, it so happened that we were discharging cases of tinned fruit and corned beef, and although the crane I was using was supposed to have only a 3-ton lifting capacity, the ship's gang were putting nearer to 5 tons on the discharging board. In fact, 3-ton Stothert & Pitt cranes were tested to lift 7 or 8 tons on the hoisting cables, so it was the electric motors in the crane that determined the lifting capacity. Most cranes were geared back so they could only lift 3 tons; this one was obviously not. A crane driver had no control over what was put onto the loading boards because the discharging gang was hundreds of feet away from him and out of his sight. The top hand was in control of the crane's movements when the crane driver was unsighted, so whatever came out of the hold, provided the crane could lift it, was what the driver had to deal with.

It happened that one set of cargo came up quite a bit heavier than the previous ones and, as I luffed it towards the crane cabin, it obviously came towards me much more slowly than the others had. I slewed the set aft and because of the extra weight, it took longer to go out when I luffed the jib aft. Consequently, the set struck the flagpole with a loud thud. There was the sound of splintering as the pole disassembled itself into matchwood on the deck. Then there was absolute silence as I strove to control the cargo over the ship's stern before taking it ashore. When I brought the crane back over the ship, I saw the flagpole had been cut off level with the stern superstructure, as cleanly as if it had been sawn off. The ship's mate and his entourage had reappeared from nowhere, as if by magic. As the crane cabin was no more than 6 feet from the ship's deck rail and almost level with the upper deck, the mate could almost confront me face to face.

He began. 'You did that deliberately,' he said. I didn't reply.

'That was criminal damage,' he said. I didn't reply.

'I'm going to report you to your company,' he said. (He was totally ignorant about the way men were employed in the docks. That is, they were only employed on a ship-by-ship basis and were not permanent staff. In fact, dockers and stevedores were picked up and paid off in the same ways as seamen – that is, they were employed only as long as they were required.)

'Could you move over a bit?' I said to him. 'I can't see my top hand.'

'Your insolence will be reported, my man,' he said.

'I'm not your man,' I replied, 'so sod off and take that crowd of gawpers with you. You're causing me to lose my concentration. Just go and see the ship worker. Tell him Henry told you to get stuffed, and don't forget to tell him I asked you to take that flagpole down.'

He did talk to the ship worker (but didn't tell him that I had asked him to take the flagpole down). Charlie told me he had had to laugh. As Charlie pointed out, with regard to running the ship, 'He doesn't even have to steer the bloody thing. They've got helmsmen to do that for them. By the way, the Governor isn't too pleased with you. That flagpole is going to cost £130 to replace. The old man has already informed the shipping company manager that he will be held responsible for what happened. At least the Governor appears to be in a forgiving mood on that score.'

The Governor may have forgiven me; the ship, she never did. Each time she came back into Tilbury Docks something untoward and unpleasant always happened to me. It had become a jinx, a bad omen. She was berthed in Tilbury Docks when I very nearly came to permanent grief, but that's another tale. Yes, the SS *Himalaya* really was the ship that never loved me.

11

ARTHUR AND THE STEAM TRAIN INCIDENT

Arthur was a big man; he wasn't very tall, but he was big. He stood about 5 feet 9 inches in height, but he had big muscles all over his body. His biceps and triceps bulged inside his coat and made it look as though the sleeves were trying to strangle his arms. When he walked, the muscles of his calves and thighs gave the impression that his trouser legs were filled with potatoes. His posterior sagged down at the back, over the tops of his legs, and his stomach bulged and hung down at the front. His jowls drooped prominently, similar to those of a bulldog. This gave him a permanent hangdog expression. He had black hair that was, or had been at odd times, combed back. He had blackish, brownish eyes set like two dates in his jelly-moulded face. His teeth were the same colour. He always had what appeared to be an obligatory three days' growth of beard. His two younger brothers resembled him in looks and manner, the poor sods.

Arthur was as strong as an ox, tough as any human being could possibly be (both physically and mentally) and as violent as an electric storm when he was upset. By nature, however, he was a gentle person. (He had an aviary in his garden where he bred canaries.) But anyone reading this tale can see that it didn't pay to rile him, not Arthur – especially if one was privy to the fact that during the Second World War he had been a physical training instructor (PTI) and an unarmed combat instructor (UCI) to British Commando units training in Scotland.

Now, I have to explain that Arthur was a loner, not a mixer. He had never worked with a regular ship's gang. This made him vulnerable to the out-of-sector allocation system used by the Dock Labour Board to supplement labour shortages in other docks within the Port of London or even in other ports, if the Board's sector manager was required to do so. It was on a very hot day in June that Arthur found himself issued with a railway warrant to take him to the King George V Dock in the upriver docks complex of the Port of London.

When he had received his orders to report to the King George V, he made his lonely way to Tilbury Town railway station on foot from the Dock Labour Board compound. There he met several other dockers who had been allocated to the same ship as him. They all got into the same compartment of an antiquated railway carriage that was to be pulled by an equally antiquated steam engine. Arthur sat in one corner while the rest of the men who managed to get a seat sat at the far end away from him. Oh, I forgot to mention that Arthur always had a sweaty smell, which wafted from him in the same way that scent exudes from flowers – it just didn't have quite the same pleasant aroma. I would say the smell emitted by our hero's torso represented more Polecat No. 5 than it did Chanel No. 5. No one who knew Arthur ever had the nerve to tell him about his aromatic condition. Well, be honest! Would you?

I have to say, it was always a very interesting exercise, travelling with one's fellow dock workers on public transport, even if it was only to observe the antics, sneers and general facial expressions of other passengers. From the time the train left Tilbury Town station till it arrived in Barking, at every stop would-be fellow-travellers looked in through the carriage window, or even managed to open the carriage door, saw that it contained what appeared to be several escaped convicts or pirates and beat a hasty retreat to another compartment. If there were passengers already in the carriage when dockers got in, several of them would get out and go to another carriage. The dockers never took umbrage at this slight because they happily sat down on the vacant seats. Those other passengers who decided to stay in the compartment when the dockers boarded generally stayed silent for the rest of the journey.

On reaching Barking station the lads changed trains. They caught another service, which took them on to Plaistow station, from where they caught a bus to the Wicket Gate outside the King George V Dock. The ship we Tilbury Dockers had been assigned to was a Blue Funnel Line vessel loaded to the gunwales with imports from India and Sri Lanka. I, for one, always thought it was bad news to be allocated to Far Eastern trading ships because of the diversity of dirty cargoes they carried. My intuition, instinct and experience were proved right when orders were received from the ship worker on our arrival.

He told us, 'The good news, lads, is that there are only 150 tons of Sri Lankan plumbago in 140-pound bags stowed in the wings of number 5 hold's upper 'tween deck. That's to be delivered to road transport. The second lot of good news is that I'm giving you a seven o'clock job and finish. It's half past ten now, so you should be finished by about five o'clock. That's the bad news: you should be on your way home in the rush hour. Right! Chop, chop! Get on with it then!' Other names for plumbago are black lead, graphite and carbon black. It is used in the manufacture of pencils or mixed with clay to make crucibles, or for polishing fireplaces, or as a lubricant and for a number of other purposes. It is a very dirty cargo. After delivering his news, the ship worker disappeared and was not seen again till we had finished discharging the plumbago. That was when he reappeared and handed our attendance books back to us, held at arm's length, the cheeky sod.

After we had been given our orders, the men separated into the various constituent groups necessary for the discharging operation to begin. Fortunately, in one respect, the ship was a stevedores' job. That means it was 'non-continuity' to us dockers and we could be paid off that night and returned to our own sector in Tilbury Docks for reallocation on the following morning's call. Or, we could be picked up for work in our own Dock Labour Board compound. It also meant there would be only one day's work. The 'job and finish' ensured the work would be completed on that day.

The top hand and the down-holders made their way onto the ship. I climbed up three tiers of vertical ladders into the crane cabin. Two of the gang remained on the quay as pitch hands, whose job it was to help the lorry drivers load their vehicles. There was a long queue of lorries on the quay ready for the direct delivery work operation. They had been waiting there since 7 a.m. and were getting rather agitated. When the dockers turned up, a few words of foul language were exchanged, and then Arthur took off his jacket and walked towards them. One couldn't be sure whether it was the Polecat No. 5 or the quivering muscles on his body that quelled any further rebellious comments, but a silence, totally devoid of even human breath or the sound of a pin falling, descended over the quay. Then Arthur, who was facing the irate drivers, waved his right thumb over his ear and ordered, in an authoritative voice reminiscent of his Sergeant PTI and UCI days in the Commandos, 'Right! Let's be having the first one of yer! Get yer lorry under 'ere.' He pointed to a spot on the quay between the railway lines close to the ship. 'Come on, now. Don't be shy. Let's be having one of yer, on the double.'

One of the drivers quickly obliged – it was obvious Arthur was not a man to be disobeyed.

In the meantime, and during the quayside altercation, the ship's gang had stripped the tarpaulins off the hatches and removed them. I had removed the

Unloading scrap metal at London Dock, April 1940. *(Tower Hamlets Local History Library)*

ship's beams and then slewed the crane ashore to pick up a set of hooks and sisal ropes, which was the gear to be used for discharging the cargo. The first lorry was driven 'under plumb' to receive bags of plumbago.

The ship's gang received 2s 11½d per ton for discharging the plumbago under the quay receiving piecework pay rates. That equated to 3d per ton per man. The plumbago was brought out of the ship's number 5 upper 'tween deck in ropes. It was made up in sets of twelve bags and was landed on the backs of lorries. It was an absolutely filthy job, and as it was a hot June day and the dockers were sweating profusely, the plumbago stuck to their clothes and skins. They were absolutely covered from head to foot in a thick black coating, except for those areas of their bodies where the sweat, running down in rivulets, showed long streaks of white flesh. Coal miners coming up from the deep pits look clean by comparison. When the Port of London mobile tea van arrived on the scene to sell refreshments, the tea lady, as the tea-van girls were known, looked at the lads and burst out laughing.

Then she said, 'I knew there was a shortage of stevedores on this berth, but I didn't know they allowed coal miners to come and do stevedores' jobs.' She quickly stopped laughing, though, when twelve pairs of eyes simultaneously turned to glare menacingly at her, before the dockers all saw the funny side of her quip and burst out laughing at themselves.

Then one of the dockers broke the ice by saying, in a put-on, sort of Oxford accent, 'Can't you see it's 'cause we are putting on our make-up to be ready for the Notting Hill Carnival.' Then, reverting to his natural voice, he said, 'What about me and the lads taking you up to the West End on a binge tonight?'

'I don't know about you lot taking me out on a binge, and what's that horrible smell? Have some of you been working on wet skins? It's more like I should get you to a public baths for a good scrub in disinfectant.' A mobile tea lady always managed to have the last word as the gangs went back to work. On this occasion she was staring directly at Arthur and puckering her nose.

'What's she staring at me for?' he said.

Bob, his workmate on the quay, rolled his eyes and said, 'She probably fancies you, Arthur! Or something.'

The gang, as the ship worker had predicted, completed the discharging operation at five o'clock in the evening. We were given our attendance books, stamped till seven o'clock as promised, and made our way home by the route we had come. There were no provisions in the docks for us to wash or clean our clothes. As we retraced our way to the Wicket Gate, the dock policeman was the first to make a comment.

'Are you lot part of the cast in the *Black and White Minstrel Show*, or are you nicking plumbago? You could all do with jumping in the dock and cleaning yourselves up, and it may get rid of that awful bloody smell, too. Ha ha ha!'

Arthur turned round menacingly and began to walk towards the policeman. 'I'll bloody ha ha ha! you in a minute,' he threatened.

The gang foreman grabbed his arm. 'Leave it, Arthur,' he said. 'We've got another 30 miles of these comments to put up with before we get back to Tilbury.' And of course he was right.

When we boarded a bus outside the dock the conductor was polite but firm. 'Don't sit on the seats, please, lads,' he said. 'If you stand in the centre aisle it will be OK for me to take you to the railway station. Otherwise I'll have to ask you all to get off the bus.'

None of the dockers argued with this request. After all, he could have asked them to leave the bus (yes, them, not me: I was the crane driver) as he had not yet issued tickets. Other passengers took no notice of us. They were obviously used to seeing dockers and stevedores plastered in all sorts of obnoxious filth that could not be removed within dock premises, simply because there were no provisions installed by the Port of London Authority for workers to do so.

After a short bus journey, we arrived at Plaistow railway station. The ticket collector was a genial black man with a great sense of humour.

'Hello, my brothers,' he said. 'Am you all from Jamaica, Trinidad or Tobago or is you one of dem black foreigners all de way from Africa? An' what brings you'm to dis godforsaken country? Am you'm all looking for de job on dis railway? Or am you a wantin' de job in the NHS? I can put de good word in for you at de Gospel Hall.'

'So what would happen when we've had a bath?' one of the gang said.

'Golly, man,' replied the ticket collector, feigning surprise. 'If you'm come out white, we'll toss you'em out. By de way, when you get in de carriage, please don't sit on de seats. It's de rush hour. All de city workers in de gents' best suits and ladies' posh dresses will be on de train.'

'Yes, all right,' replied the down-hold foreman.

As he spoke those last few words, an ancient steam train came trundling its way slowly into the station, followed somewhat reluctantly by several equally ancient carriages, a positive celebration of the genius of the great Victorian engineers.

We climbed into a compartment and the gang stood, crammed together in a line along the aisle. I, being the crane driver and the only one still without a blemish of dirt on me, sat down. One so-called city gent looked along the line of dirty, sweat-stained, tired dockers.

'Are you in charge of this filthy chain gang?' he asked me sarcastically. 'Especially that one.' He pointed to Arthur. 'He smells awful.'

All eyes turned towards the speaker; Arthur's were ablaze. He simply said to the man, 'Don't you like travelling with us?'

'No, I do not!' replied the angry passenger.

'No problem, then,' said Arthur, who was standing by the carriage door. He grabbed the so-called city gent by the scruff of the neck with one hand, as though he was picking up a mangy cat, opened the carriage door with his other hand, and tossed the offender out onto the platform, just as the train began to move out of the station. Arthur looked up and down the compartment at the other passengers.

'Is there anyone else here who don't like travelling with us?' he asked in a subdued, calm voice.

A young man, sitting on the other side of me, began to rise from his seat. I grabbed the tail of his jacket and pulled him down. He glared at me. I put my index finger to my lips and whispered in his ear, 'He's had a hard day's work, he's filthy and he's tired, and he's got a long journey home. He could kill you with a single blow. Don't push your luck, son. He may not treat you as kindly as he did that last bloke.'

The young man was wise enough to take my advice. When he got out of the carriage at Barking, he walked swiftly away and was soon out of sight. He was a very lucky lad.

When we arrived at Barking, the down-hold foreman told the dockers, 'We can't go on like this. When the next train comes in that's going to Tilbury Town, I'll have a word with the guard and ask if we can ride in the guard's van. That should stop any further antagonism with the other passengers. After all, they're right. I wouldn't want to travel with any of us in this filthy state.'

He did ask the guard, who very reluctantly agreed to let us ride with him, although it was obvious he was having second thoughts about letting Arthur share his facilities. Then he asked Arthur what I thought at the time was a very odd question.

'Do you wear sharkskin shirts?'

'As a matter of fact, I do.'

'They don't allow your skin to breathe, you know.'

'Don't they?'

'They don't,' advised the train guard.

His advice did not go unheeded. Arthur never wore sharkskin shirts to work again. I thanked the Lord for that small mercy.

12

JIM L., JOE B. AND THE LAMB INCIDENT

Jim L. and Joe B. were brothers-in-law. Jim was married to Joe's sister. It was no secret the two men hated each other, although no one knew why, only that they did and kept as far apart from each other as possible. They were similar, though, in a number of ways – just like the North and South poles.

The two brothers-in-law both worked in the same ship's gang as me. Jim was one of the two pitch hands (men who were part of the ship's gang, but worked on the quay or in lighters or barges) and Joe was the top hand (my eyes on a ship's deck). I knew Jim's face as well as I knew my own. I could see him and his mate on the pitch all day as they busied themselves with preparing cargo for loading. One or other of them was constantly looking up to see me in the crane cabin 60–80 feet above their heads, either to give me verbal orders or to make sign language that amounted to the same thing.

When Jim was bending down to his work, his black wavy hair stuck out of the yellow cravat he always wore to hide a wide, jagged scar that ran down the side of his neck. It made his hair resemble the black stigmas of a sunflower surrounded by bright-yellow petals. But as the day wore on and the sweat and dirt began to turn the yellow cravat a greasy brown colour, his head started to take on the look of a dying sunflower. That change in aspect always fascinated me. When I think of it now, it still does.

On the other hand, I could have passed Joe in the street without recognizing him. He was a lot older than Jim. Joe arrived at work at either 7 or 8 a.m., the start time depending on whether the ship was loading or discharging dry cargoes, or discharging frozen meats, cartons of offal, butter, cheeses or other chilled or frozen freight.

A normal day's loading work ran from 8 a.m. until 7 p.m. However, discharging a meat-carrying ship began at 7 a.m. and finished at 8 p.m. The reason for the earlier start and later finish was that freezer hatches were sealed with large caulk-filled plugs, which had to be removed before the ship's discharging gang could start work and then replaced at knocking-off time. The quay gang called a halt to the day's work when all the road transport lorries had been filled with frozen cargo or at 7 p.m., whichever came first. Four down-holders, the top hand and the crane driver then replugged and resealed the freezer hatch.

Loading exports for
Denmark to a liner in
Millwall Dock. (PLA
Monthly, *September 1955)*

Joe, my top hand, always made his way up onto the ship's deck as soon as he arrived at work, and that's where he stayed till lunchtime, which was midday. Before the afternoon work period began at 1 p.m., Joe would again make his way up on deck, where he remained till seven or eight o'clock in the evening. He never, ever, came down the hold for his tea break, so I never had the opportunity to get a good close-up look at his features. When the ship's gang stopped for tea, our teaboy filled an old glass bottle with tea and I brought it up onto the deck, the bottle tied to the crane's hook on a piece of looped string. This saved the old fellow having to traipse down several decks to get into the hold in order to get a drink. Anyway, we were pieceworkers: time was money and Joe knew the score.

Another reason I would not have recognized him outside the docks was simply that, when we were working, he always had his back towards me. When I brought the crane round over the ship's hold, Joe would be looking down into the open hatchway. If he wanted me to hold the set away from the hatchway, he would cross his hands over his head. If he wanted a set of cargo brought out of the hold, he would wave the fingers of his outstretched hand from his wrist with the palm facing upwards. When he wanted the load lowered, he would wave the fingers of his hand palm down. When he wanted the crane to stop, he spread the fingers of his hand and held it still. He often appeared to be giving a stage performance of a bird with one wing, although he never managed to raise himself off the ship's deck.

When Joe was waving his fingers with the palm of his hand upwards they were always in the form of a V, and I never really knew if he was trying to be downright rude or whether his arthritis was causing him pain. I also knew there was little to be gained by waving my fist at the back of his head or shouting at him. For the truth is that he would never have seen my fist, nor would he have heard my voice. All I ever saw of Joe during the ten or twelve hours we were at work each day was his back, the nape of his neck and one of his hands. I knew every wrinkle in the nape of his neck, every arthritic knuckle of his right hand. That's how I shall always remember the old fellow, my other pair of eyes.

I was the crane driver to a regular ship's gang who worked for a stevedoring contracting company. The company supplied ships and quay gangs to a number of shipping lines from men picked up on the free call (or the free-for-all as it was known among the dockers) in the Dock Labour Board compounds. The system for obtaining the services of dockers and stevedores can be likened to that of procuring prostitutes for sex. The only difference in the case of dockers was they were picked up in Dock Labour Board compounds that were kept out of the public gaze. As for stevedores, they were picked up on the stones (cobblestones in the streets outside the docks). So one could say that the only difference between stevedores and the ladies of supposedly easy virtue was that prostitutes soliciting in the streets for sex were committing a criminal offence, whereas stevedores on the stones soliciting for work were not. Why was that, I have often wondered? After all, both groups were selling physical service for money. However, I digress.

As a ship's gang discharging cargo, we were made up of one crane driver, one top hand, two pitch hands and six down-holders. On this particular day, we were working at number 1 hatch on a P&O liner that had returned from a voyage to Australia. The ship carried several hundred passengers, whose personal effects, trunks and suitcases not required on the homeward trip were stowed in the upper 'tween deck. The lower 'tween deck held bails of sheepskins and wool, which were over stowed alongside several hundred bags of letters and parcels. The lower hold, which was a freezer hold, was completely filled with sheep carcasses.

Now I have to explain that, on the day of this tale, a secondary driver had been picked up to drive the Stothert & Pitt quay crane. I had been picked up as a pro-rata man to the ship's gang. The reason for this anomaly was that I had a hospital appointment that made it necessary for me to leave the job for some hours during one of the ship's discharging days. As the ship was a luxury liner and had a limited time to stop in port, it was important for her to be discharged as quickly as possible, so she could dry dock to have her keel scraped and repainted with red lead, and her cabins, saloons and foyers stripped, revamped and restored to first-class habitable condition before she was refloated and towed by tugs to her cargo-loading and passenger-boarding berth.

It was on the fourth day of the ship's discharging that I had to attend hospital. When I returned late in the afternoon, the gang had discharged sheep and lamb carcasses from below the skeleton deck in the lower hold. They had begun to move towards the bow of the ship, some 50 feet away from the bottom of the trunkway, which was the opening to the open hatchway.

As the set of two hooks used to carry the meat nets were not long enough to reach the made-up sets of sheep carcasses in the ship's bow, a 20-foot wire pendant was attached to the hook of the crane. This was held in place by a shackle capable of holding 5 tons. The shackle was screwed to the hook of the crane. When a set of carcasses was ready to be taken out of the hold, one of the gang would go to the bottom of the hatchway and give the top hand the signal to draw the set into the centre of the ship's hold before it was hoisted up the trunkway to be landed on the meat board platform, which was set between the railway lines on the quay. On this inauspicious occasion, Jim was the man in charge of giving the signal to hoist the set. Oh! Lucky Jim!

I must confess to having arrived back at work only at about 5 p.m. after having had my nose cauterized at the hospital. I had been advised not to go into a cold atmosphere, so I went back to the ship, made my way to the lower deck, where the Goanese galley scullions had their quarters, down through the number 1 hold hatch cover into the upper 'tween deck, through the lower 'tween hatch into the skeleton deck, down the vertical ladder into the lower hold, and arrived just as the most obscene and vicious exchange of bad language erupted between the two brothers-in-law.

I will not go into detail over the obscenities, but suffice to say that the vociferous and blasphemous exchange of language almost made *me* blush. Nor do I have any idea what caused the rumpus. After all, the top hand was on deck some 100 feet away from the ceiling (bottom) of the lower hold. What I do know is that Jim waved his hand for the set of carcasses to be drawn into the centre of the hold before being hoisted up the trunkway and onto the quay. Instead, Joe stood at the top of the ship's hatchway and shouted at his brother-in-law, 'You greasy-looking, black-haired bastard, I'll bloody kill you.'

With those remarks, Joe waved his hand to the crane driver, who instantly put the crane into full hoist. The set of sheep carcasses came out of the ship's bow at top speed and shot across the lower hold like an express train. As it rose into the air, Jim, seeing the danger he was in, began to run to escape the set of sheep carcasses as it hurtled full speed towards him. Just as the set reached the centre of the hatch, he leapt up onto the bottom of the wooden skeleton deck, just as one of the frozen sheep came out of the meat net. It dropped down the side of the steel trunkway and the two hind shanks stapled Jim's foot to the wooden skeleton deck. He fell backwards and hung there, head downwards, arms outstretched, as though he was trying to mimic a circus trapeze artist.

'You stupid old bastard,' Jim screamed up at Joe. 'I've got a good claim here for compensation, and for you trying to kill me. Just wait and see what will happen when we get in court. I've got lots of witnesses. You lot saw what he did, didn't you?'

'Shut up, you stupid sod,' one of the lads said. 'You waved to Joe to take the set up. Get on with your job.'

'I can't move. I can't damn well move,' he said. Nor could he. He was stapled to the wooden framework of the skeleton deck by the shanks of the lamb.

I walked across the floor of the lower deck, climbed up into the skeleton deck, pulled Jim up into a sitting position, and prised the frozen sheep off his leg.

'I can't walk,' he complained.

'Stop that bloody moaning,' I told him, 'or I'll leave you where you are. You know how much the gang love you. They will probably book you out.' ('Booking out' meant that the gang would inform the ship worker that he wasn't working.)

I threw him over my shoulder in a fireman's hold and set about carrying him down from the skeleton deck onto the lower deck floor, then up the 30-foot ladder into the lower 'tween deck, then into the upper 'tween deck, then along the companion way that led out through the gunport door onto the quay. He never stopped griping about his brother-in-law.

'You had better wait here,' I told him. 'They've sent for an ambulance.' I made my way back through the ship and down to the lower hold, where the gang were preparing to stop work for the night.

'What have you done with Soapy?' (Jim's uncomplimentary nickname), the gang wanted to know.

'Put him on the quay.'

'You should have dumped him in the dock. What's he doing?'

'Sitting on a bollard, waiting for the ambulance.'

'He's a crafty sod. He wants a lift home. He'll be back to work in the morning at seven. He won't miss his unplugging hour's overtime if I know him,' the down-hold foreman said.

He was right. Jim turned up at 7 a.m. next day with his foot lashed into an old boot that had been cut from the tongue to the toecap. He looked like a down-at-heel retired army officer suffering from a severe bout of gout, who had escaped from the beach at Brighton and was seeking sanctuary as a stowaway in the ship's hold.

Jim's right hand was also bandaged, although nobody even mentioned that. The only comment that connected the lashed-up boot and the bandaged hand came from the down-hold foreman who said, 'I see old Joe walked into a lamppost or something last night. He's got a nasty split lip and a black eye. He should be more careful where he's walking in the dark, especially at his age.'

Jim didn't utter a word. It would appear the argument between the two brothers-in-law had been settled, at least for the present.

13

'WHAT HEROES THOU HAST BRED, ENGLAND, MY COUNTRY'

During the mid–1950s I was picked up to be employed in a quite unusual operation for a baggage gang because the gang's quay foremen had asked for the services of a crane driver. Needs must when a luxury liner is being prepared to sail, so baggage gets priority over almost everything else, especially first-class passengers' baggage.

Charlie S., the ship worker responsible for loading this particular vessel, the SS *Arcadia*, picked me up in the Dock Labour Board compound specifically to join the baggage gang of aged ex-warriors who were employed by Scrutton's Stevedoring Company Limited to receive passengers' forward baggage on behalf of the Pacific & Orient Line.

The baggage gang was made up of 'B' men (those still reporting for work in Dock Labour Board compounds who were past the state retirement age of 65). Most were in their late sixties and seventies, but there were a few octogenarians thrown in for good measure. It is difficult to describe those old men accurately in their demeanour and attitude because they hardly spoke to each other, let alone to a stranger such as myself. When they did respond, however, their manner was belligerently hostile, and their demeanour pugnaciously offensive. They always appeared to be ready to square up for a fight. Mostly, too, if they spoke, their voices were as vitriolic as a sergeant major's bellowing at raw recruits on a parade ground. We young dockers called them the old grousers, though most of us knew them for what they really were: the veterans of battles and wars that had long since passed into history. They were Britain's forgotten (or ignored) heroes – the docks all round the British Isles still employed quite a few of them. They were men who had fought in the Boer War and the First World War. They were men whom the enemy had failed to kill on the battlefields. But that didn't alter the fact that they really were old grousers, and that their deeds of long, long ago, performed in their youthful years, now counted for very little in the country for which they had fought, and possibly even less in an industry where, during the 1940s, '50s and '60s, almost every man was a veteran of some conflict or other.

Empire Parkeston. *(Author's collection)*

Before I left the Dock Labour Board compound to make my way to the southern quay, Tilbury Docks, I was told by Charlie that I would probably be treated as though I was suffering from leprosy when I got to where the old grousers of the baggage gang were working. He was right.

'What do you want, sonny?' I was asked by the baggage gang foreman, a grey-haired, grey-faced, grey-eyed, wizened-skinned, round-shouldered remnant of a bygone age, who looked as though he had been recently dug up in the local churchyard, dusted down with a stiff brush and sent back to work in the docks.

'I'm here as the pro-rata crane driver to the baggage gang,' I told him.

He looked me up and down, glaring at me with those piercing grey eyes of his. Then slowly, with the cold, self-controlled deliberation of a praying mantis, he took a snuff box out of his waistcoat pocket and with well-practised mechanical movements, he opened it, took out a pinch of snuff with his index finger and thumb, raised it to his nose, sniffed some of it up each nostril in turn, gave an almighty sneeze, shook his head, blinked a couple of times, looked me up and down and said, 'You're a bit young to be a crane driver aren't you, sonny?'

'I drive the Stothert & Pitt quay crane at number 1 hatch on P&O boats for Charlie S.,' I told him.

He looked at me in utter surprise. 'Do you?' he said. 'Then you'll have to do, I suppose. I've got a heavy lift coming by lorry that's got to go onto a low-loader. It won't be here for some time. The baggage gang are working out of rail trucks at the back door. They'll find you something to do to amuse yourself till the heavy lift turns up, or they'll let you know when they want you.' With those last few words he disappeared among the cargo in the transit shed and I never saw him again. (It did cross my mind that he may have returned to his coffin in a churchyard somewhere.)

I made my way to the rear doors of the transit shed where the old grousers were busily moving crates, suitcases and boxes of personal effects from rail trucks into the shed on wheelbarrows. There they sorted them out into their various ports for discharge and colour-coded each item accordingly.

At first I stood by an open doorway watching those agile old men enter a rail truck one at a time to have their wheelbarrow loaded. Then they slowly pulled their barrow backwards off the truck, over a toe-board and onto the cargo bank, before pushing the load into the transit shed to be sorted and placed in its correct stowage. I watched them for some time, listening to their occasional humorous banter or the vitriolic remarks they made to one another. It was always amusing to them when one of their number dropped a suitcase or some other package and had to pick it up; and there was always vitriolic language when one of them fell out of the line to relieve himself because of 'water-works trouble'.

I was so engrossed that I was shaken when a voice behind me shouted in my ear, 'And what the bloody hell do you want, sonny?'

I turned round quickly to see one of the old grousers standing behind me. He was holding a large old battered brown enamelled teapot, and he was glaring at me through a pair of thick-rimmed spectacles with what can only be described as an opprobrious look in his eyes.

'Oh,' I said. 'I'm your crane driver. I've come to take a heavy lift off a lorry when it turns up.'

It was his turn to look surprised. 'You're a bit young to be a crane driver, aren't you, sonny?'

'Am I?' I said. 'That's exactly what your foreman asked me.' And before the old grouser had a chance to say anything else, I said, 'I've been driving a high-flyer Stothert & Pitt quay crane for the ship's gang at number 1 hatch on Pacific & Orient liners for the past two years.'

'Hmm, have you?' he grunted. Then he asked me, 'Do you want a mug of tea? It's beer-oh time.'

'Yes, that will be nice,' I replied.

'Then you had better go and nick a PLA mug. I've only got enough for the baggage gang. We'll knock off for beer-oh as soon as they've emptied that last rail truck. Then we'll have to wait for a while till the next shunt of trucks are brought in. That'll take at least half an hour.' He continued, 'The tea's twopence a mug or sixpence all day. You can pay me when I pour the tea, right?'

Who was I to argue with that belligerent old blighter? 'Yes, OK,' I replied.

I made my way onto the quayside where the Port Authority mobile tea van always parked to serve refreshments to the dockers, lightermen and lorry drivers. I found an empty mug and went back to the baggage gang where the old grousers were assembled in a small group, sitting almost in silence, except that is for the slurping of tea and the munching of sandwiches, at which they were gnawing with badly fitting false teeth. It was an experience that was best appreciated with closed eyes. Then one could imagine, without too much effort, that one was listening to a team of Spanish flamenco dancers going through one of their more energetic and rumbustious fandango routines, with the full use of castanets and the occasional accompaniment of intermittent bursts from the rumbling of kettle-drums (or even a runaway horse clip-clopping downhill at high speed).

One of the old grousers looked at me several times with half-closed eyes before he finally spoke. 'Old Ted's boy, aren't you?'

'No,' I replied. 'Ted was my grandfather.'

'I thought there was a family resemblance. You've got that sullen dog-in-the-manger depressed look about you.'

'So would you have if you were me,' I told him, 'being sent here to work with you miserable lot of old sods.'

He laughed, and then said, 'How's your grandfather?'

'He's all right,' I replied. 'He's retired now. He left the docks in 1940 when he was 69. My grandmother didn't want him sent to Wales or Scotland by the Dock Labour Corporation. He went to work for the general manager of the Imperial Paper Mills as his gardener when he left the docks. He packed it in when he was

SS *Goldfinch* at berth at London Dock. *(Industries of Stepney, Metropolitan Borough of Stepney, 1948)*

75 when my grandmother died.'

'Good for him,' was the reply. 'It must be nice to be able to retire while you're still young enough to enjoy life.' The old man said it with a smile on his face. 'By the way,' he continued, 'my name's Jack. The lads call me Jacko.'

'Had you known my grandfather very long, Jack?' I asked him.

'Since the end of the First World War when I came to work in the docks,' he replied. 'I served with your father in the Royal West Kents in France during that war. We were lucky to come out of that lot alive, I'll tell you. We were both wounded in the first battle of the Somme in July 1916. We both got blighty wounds. Your dad was hit by a splinter of shrapnel that went through the back of his hand; I stopped a bullet with my leg. Saved our lives those wounds did. If it hadn't been for them wounds, we would never have survived the First World War, your dad and me.'

'Listen to that young whippersnapper,' said one of the two octogenarians. 'First World War was a bloody picnic compared to the Boer War. We wasn't loafing about in trenches out on the veldt in the Boer War, and having the odd game of football against the Boers, like you lot were doing with the Germans in France. No bloody fear. We were marchin' across the veldt chasing the bloody Boers, and when we caught up with them, the blighters opened up on us with their rifles, and bloody crack-shots they all were. They decimated our ranks they did. Didn't they, Harry?'

Harry, the other octogenarian, didn't reply, but went on gnawing, with some difficulty, at his sandwich.

The first octogenarian shouted at Harry. 'Are you in today, you deaf old sod, or are you trying to ignore me?'

Harry looked up from his sandwich with some relief at being given respite from what was plainly a physical exertion on his part – the effort of simply watching him chewing was making me feel tired. But even when Harry stopped gnawing, his false teeth kept moving in his jaw, as though they were waiting for an order to stand down. As the order didn't come, the teeth took it upon themselves to lose momentum very slowly and they finally came to a stop. Then he asked, 'What's that you said, Sid?'

'I said the First World War was a bloody picnic compared with the Boer War,' replied the first octogenarian.

'Was it?' said Harry. 'I couldn't say. I got wounded in the Boer War and was classed as unfit for military service for the First World War, but I did join the Local Defence Volunteers in the Second World War – that's before Winston Churchill called it the Home Guard.'

'I know you was wounded in the Boer War, you silly old blighter,' said Sid. 'That's what I'm saying. We were both shot-up in the Boer War. It stands to reason it must have been worse than the First World War. Do you remember when we enlisted in 1899 and were sent to Aldershot?'

'Yes,' said Harry. 'Then we were sent to join the 1st Battalion, Essex Regiment, weren't we?'

'Yes, that's right,' said Sid, 'the old 44th/56th of Foot, the Essex and the Wessex.'

'Yes, 1899, or was it 1900 when we sailed for South Africa from Liverpool? Or was it Southampton? My memory isn't as good as it was.'

'Mine neither, but it was one of those two ports, I think,' said Sid.

It was then that Sid went into a sort of daze or daydream. A period of absolute silence descended over the baggage gang, except for the slurping of tea, burping stomach gasses, gnashing teeth and the passing of excess wind that escaped through some rectums as loudly as if it were being discharged from a jet aircraft engine. Then Sid came back to reality.

'I think it was 1899 that we embarked on a White Star liner at Liverpool docks, bound for the Cape. I remember there were other regiments aboard – the Gloucesters and the Scottish Rifles and a field hospital of the RAMC. If I remember correctly, we were at sea for three weeks before arriving at Cape Town. When we had docked Lord Kitchener came aboard to inspect *his* troops before we were allowed to disembark. Do you remember? We were drawn up in ranks of four on the quay, and then we were marched to a transit camp, where we spent several days before being entrained at Cape Town railway station. Our destination, we thought, was to be the Orange River where we were supposed to arrive after two days' travelling.'

'Yes,' piped up Harry. 'What a bloody horrible journey that was, Sid, wasn't it? But at least it had one consolation.'

'Did it?' said Sid in utter surprise. 'What was that?'

'Now who's a silly old sod,' said Harry. 'Because we didn't have to march all the bloody way there, did we?'

'No, I make you right there, Harry,' said Sid reluctantly (apparently Sid never liked Harry to be one up on him). 'Anyway,' he continued, 'we were dropped off the train at a station somewhere along the railway line to join Lord Roberts's forces, just as he was preparing to close in on a place called Paardeberg, wasn't we, Harry?' said Sid, seeking confirmation as to the factual contents of his tale. It was a statement to which Harry nodded his agreement, although I'm not sure he had heard one word Sid had said, and Sid himself was obliviously lost in his past as he continued talking about the events that culminated in the battle of Modder River.

'We was with a troop of mounted infantry, not far from Paardeburg Drift, when the Boers began sniping at us. But they couldn't have known we were within the sound of gunshot of the 6th Division, who instantly came to our assistance when they heard gunfire. When the 6th Division came up to us the Boers took off, and we waited about for some time before our CO, Colonel Stephenson, marched us (the 1st Battalion, Essex Regiment and the 1st Battalion, Welch Regiment) right out onto the veldt, and had us deployed opposite the river below Koodoosrand Drift. There were some of the best fighting soldiers on this earth in the 6th Division – the West Yorks, and the Highland Brigade who had come down onto the veldt from of the Kliproal Road. We were ordered to spread out on the left of General Knox's brigade with the Argyll and Sutherland Highlanders on the right, the Black Watch in the centre, and the Seaforth Highlanders on their left. The Highland Light Infantry was left at Klip Drift to protect the lines of communications.'

'Tell them about Kitchener's bold plan, Sid. You know, his Iron Fist theory.'

'Oh, yes,' said Sid, 'the Iron Fist theory; well, that's what the army lads chose to call it. In fact the object of Kitchener's plan, if it could be called a plan, was to

Captain Davis (right) taking over as the river pilot from Captain Brown, the sea pilot, of the RMS *Highland Brigade*, *c*. 1938. *(Author's collection)*

throw all his available infantry into a battle. The Boer commander was a bloke we called Old Cronje, and unbeknown to us, the old sod had almost got his Boer Army encircled. Lord Kitchener wanted to close the only gap through which the Boers could escape, but of course we Tommies weren't privy to Kitchener's plans. What's more he wasn't too concerned how many of us Tommies he got killed in the process. From our experience of fighting the Boers, we all knew it was going to be blood, flesh and bone against well-aimed bullets from their Mauser and Martini-Henry rifles.

'The 1st Essex and the 1st Welch were part of Stephenson's 18th Brigade, and our job was to hold the Boers with a frontal assault from the veldt to the south, but as far as we infantrymen were concerned, we wasn't sure whether we were holding them down, or they were just using us as target practice. Whatever it was they didn't escape past us, that's for sure. Wasn't it, Harry?'

'What's that you said, Sid?'

'It doesn't matter, Harry. Give it a miss.' Then he said, 'The bloody deaf old sod. He's been like that since the Boer War. Deaf as a post in his right ear. God only knows why.'

'Could it have been due to the constant firing of his rifle alongside his right ear?' I tentatively suggested to Sid.

'Why should it have been?' Sid barked at me. 'I'm not like it.'

'Aren't you,' I said, lowering my voice to almost a whisper.

'What did you say, sonny,' Sid grunted, his eyes lighting up with indignation.

I raised my voice a couple of decibels and repeated. 'Could it have been that firing his rifle from his right shoulder brought about his deafness?'

'Why should it have been?' said Sid. 'I'm not deaf like him.' Then he went on, 'Anyway, what was I saying?'

'Something about crossing the veldt,' I reminded him.

'Yes, the open veldt. We were ordered to press on across the open veldt. We were tired, hungry and thirsty. We had been on half-rations for days on end, and we'd been on the march since five o'clock (1700 hours) the previous day without even a chance to fill our water bottles. Then, as we came over a rise, below us in a great circle was Old General Cronje's wagon train. The sight of those covered wagons bucked us up no end. We thought that once we got down among them, we'd at least get some fresh water and grub. Didn't we, Harry?'

'Oh, yes,' Harry agreed, as he prepared to set his jaws in motion for another concerted attack on his almost impregnable sandwich.

'Why don't you dip that sandwich in your tea, you stupid sod?' one of the other old grousers suggested. 'At least it will soften up the bread and lubricate those teeth of yours.'

Harry appeared not to hear the remark (or chose not to), and he continued to gnaw away at the slowly diminishing sandwich in his hand; a sandwich that had started out as two slices of bread and something, but was now a round ball of what appeared to be dough and something. He was gnawing away as though his life depended on it. The spectacle was enough to make any weak-stomached person vomit – including me.

Sid, in the meantime, had continued with his narrative: 'We (the Essex and the Welch) were the first to be sent into the attack, but the Boers were ready and waiting for us, and we suffered heavy casualties from their snipers who pinned us down on the open veldt, picking us off one by one – that's when Harry and me stopped a bullet each. Didn't we, Harry?'

Harry looked up from his bread and something through half-closed eyes, eyes that now glowed with menace and hatred. 'Yes, Sid,' he replied. 'Those bloody generals were so intent on winning the battle, they didn't give a damn about how many of their own men they got killed. We were lucky though, weren't we, Sid? We were shot in the chest, both of us. We've both shunted along on one lung ever since. Generals they called themselves; assassins more like. They were so keen on winning battles, didn't care how many men they got killed, did they, Sid?'

'No, old mate, they didn't,' Sid said.

After Harry's verbal tirade there was a deep silence. It was a silence occasionally broken by the sound of tea being slurped from refilled PLA mugs and the rumbling of ancient stomachs. There was also the painful creaking of old bones that were soon to be reactivated when the old grousers returned to the tedious task of unloading more baggage from more railway trucks. Until then, all was as quiet as the graves these old grousers would soon be occupying.

I couldn't help but look along the line of them with admiration. What terrible sights they had seen and been party to. What privations they had been through in wars, and the old sods would still take you on in a fight. Here they were, still working in the docks, all because there was no occupational pension for them and the state pension was insufficient to live on. A hymn that I sang during assembly in my school days came into my mind:

> What heroes thou hast bred, England, my country,
> I see the mighty dead, march in line,
> Each with undaunted heart, playing his gallant part,
> Made England what thou art, Mother of mine.

Now England had deserted them, her sons, left them to work out their last years doing hard labour till the day they died. There was no Elizabeth Fry of the Society of Friends (the prison reformer), or Jeremy Bentham (the eighteenth/nineteenth-century Utilitarian philosopher) to argue their case for socio-economic justice. There was a trade union, but that organization was under continuous attack by the press and other media for trying to improve their lot. So, like the old soldiers they had been, and the old grousers they had become, they worked on and on till in God's own good time, one by one, they faded away.

I shall always remember Sid and Harry. The thing I recall most vividly about them is that after their long tirade about the Boer War, the two old fellows, sitting side by side, began to sing this song, which had been written by a couple of their comrades in Carnarvon Hospital, South Africa. They called it 'It Takes a Lot to Make a Fellow Smile', and it went like this:

> I don't go in for sentiment, it isn't in my line,
> 'cause it only makes a fellow get the hump.
> Especially when he's fighting and a-bobbing up and down,
> Lucky not to get a Boer bullet in his rump.
> But sometimes I get to thinking, of the missus at the tub,
> Where I guess as every day she can be seen.
> A-washing shirts and such like, to buy a bit of grub,
> To feed our kiddies, the children, of the soldiers of the Queen.

> *Chorus*
> No! It isn't the blooming fighting, or the laying out at night,
> With ants a-crawling all around your blooming dial.
> But it's wondering if the missus and the kids can be all right,
> That's why it takes such a lot to make a fellow want to smile.

> Now here's a letter from my Sarah, of about a month ago,
> And it seems as if she's writing in a blooming tiff.
> For she wants to know the reasons, why they're making such a fuss,
> And how she'd like to talk to this 'ere '*Lady Smith*'.

Dunbar Wharf. *(Tower Hamlets Local History Library)*

She was always kind o' jealous, but she's still a proper mate,
And when I writes explaining to her what is what.
And tells her there's no 'Lady-Killing' out here at any rate,
Why, with joy she'll go clean fairly off her dot.

Chorus
No! It isn't the blooming petticoats, they're things we never see,
And to go a–courting of the locals isn't just the style.
But when I think as how the missus might go divorcing me,
Why, it takes a lot to make a fellow want to smile.

Now she tells me that the people, living round our show,
Have started calling me such nasty names.
And they says that I'm an absent-minded beggar, which of course,
Makes her up and want to know their little games.
Why, I'm always thinking of her and our chubby little kids,
And I'll write and let her know I'm just as straight.
As the day that we were married, and I'll send her home some quids,
Just to show her I don't forget my dear old mate.

Chorus
Course it kinds of hurts my feelings, and a lump gets in my throat,
To say I'm absent minded isn't quite the style,
And when it comes to thinking, I may never make the boat
That's due to take me home, why it takes a lot to make a soldier smile.

Sid and Harry's venture back into memory lane was soon ended by the arrival of a lorry carrying the heavy lift that I had been sent to deal with. It turned out to be a vintage car in a wooden crate and it weighed about 2 tons. It took me no more than a few minutes to climb up the three flights of steel ladders into the Stothert & Pitt quay crane, slew the jib over the wooden crate, and lift it off the lorry and lower it onto a low-loader ready to be put aboard the SS *Arcadia*. I then, without so much as a by-your-leave to the baggage gang, made my way to Scrutton's office and retrieved my attendance book. I never ever saw the old grousers again. But over the years I've often thought of Sid, Harry, Jack and the other old fellows I worked with, and of what they had gone through in their long lives; of how much their country had taken from them, and how little it had been prepared to give them back in return, to its everlasting shame.

14

GEORGE'S LAST WAGER

'Is it still raining, George?' The question came from Bert, the ship's down-hold foreman, and was addressed to one of the bargehands to Bert's ship's discharging gang. George was standing inside a transit shed doorway, leaning against one of its steel support stanchions, holding his docker's hook in his left hand, swearing and cursing the weather, as he watched the raindrops falling in an almost continuous sheet across the quayside, running in a stream down the ship's derrick before bouncing off the deck and the hatch covers of the SS *Ebo*, a vessel owned by the Elder Dempster shipping line.

The SS *Ebo* was a passenger and cargo liner that traded between the Port of London's Tilbury Docks and pre-selected ports down the West African coast from Dakar in Senegal to Luanda in Angola. The ship was secured fore and aft to her discharging berth in Tilbury Docks by wire hawsers and nylon ropes attached to cast-iron bollards concreted into the quay. From her cargo holds only an hour before the ship's down-hold gangs had begun to discharge cocoa beans into Thames lighters for that expensive commercial commodity's final lap in its sea voyage, upriver to the import merchants' processing factories.

The West African cocoa beans were to be transported to a destination in east London, where they would undergo the process of fermentation, followed by roasting, after which they would be ground down into a fine powder and used in making chocolate and other food and drink products. It was of paramount importance that the cocoa beans should not become prematurely wet or damp during the discharging operation, simply because they quickly begin to deteriorate. So the rain inevitably brought an abrupt stoppage in the discharging operation. And the rainstorm was building up a bout of mental and physical aggression in George. (For the benefit of the reader of this tale, the over-side discharging piecework rate paid to dockers for carrying out this particular operation was 3*s* 1*d* per ton per ship's gang.)

'Yes, it's still damn raining,' George replied, 'and it won't bloody stop this morning by the looks of it. Sod it.' And he walked further into the transit shed, keeping himself distanced from the other gang members.

George wasn't a man to waste words, and what he had just said was generally more than his speech quota for a whole day. He was an odd sort of character, with

Limehouse Reach,
November 1949. *(John
Topham Picture Library)*

a curious antisocial disposition, who didn't appear to like or even to trust other
people – he was a maverick who always kept his fellow dockers at a distance, never
making friends. George was a loner with a grudge, and it was obvious he could be
a very dangerous man if he was antagonized.

To describe a man such as George is difficult: he was sort of short to medium
in height, that is, he stood about 5 feet 7 inches. He weighed something like 14
stone. He had deep bluish–greyish eyes and a pug nose, which showed it had
received a thump or two in boxing rings or in street brawls. Sadly, all his facial
features appeared to have been etched onto a large mangelwurzel-shaped head, a
concoction that was capped with a mop of black wavy hair that was going grey
around his ears and neck, a feature, oddly enough, that enhanced the
magnificence of his ugliness. As one wag had suggested, he could have made more
money being exhibited in a chamber of horrors than he would ever see working as
a wage slave in the docking industry.

Finally, in addition to his unfortunate cosmetic appearance, there were his
physical deformities, including rounded shoulders that caused his head to hang
over his chest, reminiscent of Neolithic man. He had long arms that bulged with
muscles and that, from the rear, gave him the appearance of a gorilla. On the end

of the arms were two huge hands. Had they been yellow, anyone would have been forgiven for mistaking them for two bunches of bananas.

He looked what he was: a tough, vindictive character with a grudge against society as a whole and no individual in particular, who was always on the look-out for a fellow protagonist with whom, or on whom, he could vent his intense, built-up aggression. That, I must advise the reader, was a problem in the docking industry, where virtually every man had been trained as an assassin by instructors employed for that purpose within His Majesty's armed services.

'The ship's mate isn't likely to order us to take off the beams and hatches again in this weather,' Bert said. 'What about playing a hand or two of cards? It will help to pass the time away till the rain stops.' There was a mutter of approval from several members of the ship's gang, who came forward and volunteered to play, seven in fact. That almost made up two sets of players, but they were still one man short.

'We need one more man for a game of cards,' Bert called out, but nobody else came forward to play.

'What about you, Terry?' Terry was our resident Communist Party gang member, with degrees in political economics and philosophy. He looked up from scrutinizing the contents of his *Daily Worker* newspaper, sneered down his nose, gave Bert a look of utter contempt, and carried on reading.

Bert shrugged his shoulders and then said, 'What about you, George? A game of cards to pass the time away?'

'No, not me,' George growled, slowly shaking his mangelwurzel-shaped cranium.

'Why not?' Bert taunted him. 'I've come to believe there's something very odd about you. Come to think about it, I've never seen you have a bet on the dogs or horses. In point of fact, I've never seen you have a bet at all, not even in Smoky Joe's Café. You won't even play a hand of cards. Are you afraid of losing your money?'

George walked over to the card school group and, raising his big fist, firmly jabbed a banana-sized index finger into Bert's chest. He said, 'Nothing you could do would frighten me.'

Bert, who had been sitting down, suddenly stood up. He was several inches taller than George, and as powerfully built. He glared down at the smaller man.

'If that's the case, get your money out and play, you tight-fisted little sod.' His attitude was threatening.

George's eyes narrowed, then he said, 'I used to be an idiot like you lot. If anything I was more addicted to gambling than all you lot put together. I used to take wagers on anything.'

'So what brought about your cure from that addiction?' Bert said and laughed. 'A trip to Lourdes, was it? Or perhaps it was a long psychiatric session with Sigmund Freud on the way we see ourselves? Or was it because you woke up one night from having had a dream about heaven, and thought that you'd seen the light of God? Or is it simply because you really are a tight-fisted, miserly little sod?'

Blood was about to be spilled. Then one of the other gang members quickly broke into the verbal confrontation with, 'So what cured you of the gambling habit, George?'

George sat down on a tea chest and began to tell us this story. It was as though he had been waiting for years to unload his burden onto someone because the words of his tale came out of his mouth so naturally.

'It's funny how some people meet, isn't it? I mean, meeting different people appears to be coincidental to most of us, but I'm sure that in most instances it's fate that brings us together for specific purposes. Now, take my case as an example. I first met my mate John Broomfield at Colchester Army Barracks in March 1940. We had both recently been conscripted into the army. He was an East End Londoner and I was from Dagenham, Essex. I knew his manor around Stepney pretty well because I was a van boy and worked for the Co-operative Wholesale Society, and our department made deliveries in east London, but John (except for his family's 'op pickin' 'olidays down in Kent) had never been farther than Woolwich before he had been called up for military service, and that was only because he and his mates used to cross the river on the Woolwich free ferry when they was a kids.

'We hit it off right away, John and I. In fact I doubt if two young men had ever been more alike, without being identical twins, that is. We thought alike, we liked the same sort of things, we even looked alike, and we both had a mania for gambling. The other lads in our training squad used to rib us about it. They reckoned one of our dads had had a roving eye, and to have looked at us I'm sure they must have been right.'

'Bloody hell,' Bert blurted out. 'There can't be another freak walking about looking like you, can there?'

George either didn't hear the outburst or ignored it. He continued, 'But the one thing we were both mostly attracted to was gambling, and it was the gambling bug that parted us in the end.'

'How did that come about?' asked one of the gang.

'Well, after we had been at the army training camp for a few weeks, we had become recognized as the unit's bookmakers. We would take bets on anything or anyone; for example, who would be first to be absent without leave, who'd be in the first overseas draft. You know the sort of thing I mean. Once we even took bets with a whole platoon that we could get our sergeant to miss what they all thought was his favourite sport, that was turning over our newly laid-out clean and blancoed kit, when he did his daily inspection.

'The sergeant was an old regular and had served in the army since the First World War. That, as it turned out, was to our advantage, because it allowed us to lengthen the betting odds in our favour. What we had to do first was to find the sergeant's weak points in order to achieve our purpose. John and I, when we were cleaning our kit, racked our brains for the solution to the problem. Then John suddenly hit on a brilliant idea:

'"I've got it, George," he said. "You leave it to me, mate; just leave it to me." He got up and, hee-hawing like a donkey with a bunch of fresh carrots, he virtually threw himself out of our marquee (the big tent that was our temporary home till we had finished our basic training), as though all the dogs of hell were at his heels.

'On the following day the kit inspection was carried out as per usual, but by a second lieutenant and a corporal. Our illustrious sergeant was noticeable by his absence. I couldn't think how our luck had been so quick in coming, because when John had arrived back in the marquee, he hadn't said anything more to me about the affair, although after the sergeant's absence from the kit inspection he had happily collected our winnings during blanco time in the marquee.

'Then, when we were sitting on our bunks, cleaning our brasses and blancoing our webbings the following evening, the sergeant appeared at the entrance:

'"'ten-shun," the sergeant's voice bellowed out. We shot up from our bunks onto our feet and stood like ramrods waiting for his next kind words.

'"Right," he roared. "Which one of you clever young bastards sent me a telegram saying my wife had just given birth to twins?"

'Not one word was uttered by any of the men in the marquee, but their eyes all slowly worked their way towards the corner of their sockets, which was in John's and my direction. The sergeant's eyes followed them.

'"Oh, so it was you young pair of bastards, was it? Get over to my office on the double. Now!" he shouted at the top of his voice. John and I went out through the marquee flap with the speed of light infantrymen, and with the sergeant bellowing behind us, "Left right, left right, left right," till we got up to his office door. "Halt," he yelled (which was just as well, otherwise we would have had to try marching through the wooden walls of the building) and we stood marching on the spot till he opened the hut door and barked the order, "Get inside."

'We marched into his office and stood to attention in front of his desk. He followed us in and walked round us, sizing us up before he sat down. His eyes didn't leave us for a second.

'"Right now! What's your flaming game?" he demanded to know. I left it to John to explain. After John had told him about the bets we had taken on with the platoon, and the need for "his good self" to be absent from the kit inspection, the sergeant's face broke into a crafty smile and he winked at us.

'"Oh," he said, "that's all it was then, a bit of a caper, eh – boyish prank, no harm meant and no damage done?" he suggested.

'"That's right, Sergeant," said John. "No 'arm meant. It was just for a bet."

'"Oh I see. Just for a jolly old wager, was it? By the way, how much did you make at my expense?" the sergeant demanded to know, his eyes narrowing into what was a positive threat.

'"Twenty quid, Sergeant," John replied.

'"Hmm, now," he said. "I'm a gambling man myself and like to have a wager occasionally, so this is what I'll do. I bet you two twenty quid that, if I report this prank of yours to the CO, you will both get six months in a glass house. You may think I'm a hard disciplinarian, but you wait till those Red Caps get hold of you in a military prison. Then you'll think I've been giving you the kid-glove treatment."

'John, as quick as a flash, dived his hand into his tunic pocket and brought out four £5 notes. "No need for that, Sergeant. We accept that bet," John said, and placed the money on his desk.

'"It's a wager then," the sergeant said, and picked up the cash.

'"Yes, you're on, Sergeant," John replied, and made to shake hands on the deal. The sergeant ignored John's hand.

'"Get out of here, and don't you ever try any of those tricks on me again, or I'll have the pair of you roasted alive. Get me?" He was roaring at us as though he was a mad bull.

'We didn't wait for a second longer, just in case he changed his mind. We went out of his office faster than a pair of greyhounds rounding the bend at a White City race meeting. When we had got back in the marquee, we dropped down on our bunks gasping for breath and wheezing like a pair of old steam engines. When I'd got my breath back, I said to John, "I thought we had made thirty quid on those bets?"

'"Yes, George, we did, but the sergeant wasn't to know that, was he? He may have got twenty quid, but at least we got a fiver each," and putting his hand once again into his tunic pocket, he passed me a nice, crisp, white £5 note.

'"Well, at least we managed to salvage something out of those bets we took on, John," I told him. "By the way, I thought the sergeant was a bit upset about those twins you fostered onto him, didn't you?"

'"So would you have been if you was him," John winked. "You see, when I left you the day before yesterday, I made a few enquiries about our sergeant. I discovered his wife was living in army married quarters near Kidbrook in Kent. What's more, the sergeant had been abroad in India for twelve months and had only had his first leave six months ago. I telephoned one of my mates in the East End. He works on the south side of the Thames just outside Blackwall Tunnel, and he sent a telegram for me to the sergeant here at Colchester Barracks, telling

The Tilbury-to-Gravesend steam ferry, *Rose*, approaching Gravesend town pier, 1950s. *(Author's collection)*

him his wife had had twins. The sergeant was given instant compassionate leave, and shot off home as fast as a bullet from a rifle, no doubt with murder on his mind. That's what got him away from the kit inspection." John looked through the marquee flap entrance, back towards the sergeant's office. Then he said, "I always thought that sergeant was a real callous bastard, but he had us bang to rights just now, and he let us off. I won't forget that in a hurry."

'"It cost us twenty quid just the same," I pointed out.

'John winked and said, "We'll have to put that down to wetting the babies' heads, won't we?" and laughed.

'He was a fine fellow and a good mate was John,' George said softly. 'And I never placed another bet in my life.'

The ship's gang had been silenced by George's tale, and they sat for some minutes before continuing their round of cards, spellbound as Bert and George walked off along the dock quay, heading for the public house known to all dock workers as the top canteen.

15

OLD DAVE AND THE SCOTCH WHISKY INCIDENT

O ld Dave, as he was universally known in the docks, was in his mid-60s. He had been a docker since leaving the Royal Navy in 1919, almost forty years earlier. He was close to the state retirement age of 65. That meant nothing to dockers in those days, simply because the state retirement pension was totally inadequate for working-class people to live on. Neither was there a contributory works pension scheme for registered port workers that could produce extra funds to augment the derisory state benefit. Therefore, apart from being relegated to a 'B' man's status (the over-65 'A' and 'C' men who had their fall-back guarantee reduced from eleven turns to four turns each week till they left the industry), the old fellow could go on offering his services on the free call to ship workers and quay foremen all eleven turns each working week until the day he died – and like most of them, he did.

Dave was a veteran of the First World War and it showed. He had never enlightened anyone as to which branch of the Royal Navy he had served in, but it was obvious from his perpetually nervous state that it had been dangerous. He was always on edge, fraught and shaky. Nevertheless, he was a lovely old man in every way, the sort of chap anyone would wish to have as a grandfather. (I hasten to add that my own grandfather was of the same benign disposition. They were both Mr Pickwick-type characters.

Dave wasn't very tall, about 5 feet 7 inches, but he was rotund. He was not obese, just nicely rounded. Only when he removed his cap, which wasn't very often when he was working, could one see he was bald on top. The bald part, which was shiny and red, looked as if it had been waxed, and the grey hairs that circled his cranium, almost from eye to eye, gave the top of his head the appearance of the sun rising through a grey morning mist when he bent down. Well, at least it did to me.

Dave was a docker of the old school, a quietly spoken man, when he spoke at all, which wasn't very often. He always came to work wearing a dark suit with a waistcoat, in the pocket of which he sported a silver watch. The watch was attached to a silver chain and an Albert, which was anchored in place to a buttonhole in the waistcoat. In his lapel would be a flower, which he removed on the quay and let gently fall into the dock each morning. No one ever asked him why he did that. Nor did he ever volunteer to tell. Whatever his reason, it was something personal. A ritual.

Dave was on the Port Authority 'A' list of dockers – that is, dockers who were allocated to jobs by the Port Authority labour master from the Dock Labour Board compound. (They were not to be confused with 'A' 'B' and 'C' category dockers as listed for work purposes by the Dock Labour Board manager; those men did jobs that had not been manned by perms.)

Old Dave and I had been sent to work with a freight-striking gang. Striking gangs were made up of eight men, six to push handheld wheelbarrows and two to load the barrows with cases, cartons or other packages. Our gang had been assigned the job of striking freight from rail trucks. The rail trucks carried mixed loads of cartons and cases all of sizes, shapes and weights destined for various Australian ports as cargo on a P&O liner. Dave and I were given the job of breaking out the freight and loading the hand-propelled barrows for the men who would remove the struck goods from the rail trucks into their respective bays in the transit shed. The scene is now set.

We removed the tarpaulin covers from of the rail trucks, folding each one before we cleared the freight. Then, having removed the cases and packages, we put the folded tarpaulin cover back in each truck. We had progressed down the shunt, having unloaded about a dozen trucks before the mid-morning tea break. We had struck some 40 tons of dead-weight cargo – a large proportion of the goods were lightweight cartons and cases, of little value to us as we were paid by the dead-weight ton. Then we came to a truck of Scotch whisky, Black Label. Old Dave's eyes lit up.

'I could do with a drink,' he said. They were the first words he had spoken all morning.

'There's about 300 cases here.' I replied. 'Help yourself.'

'How do I get one open?'

'Christ, Dave! You've been working here for forty years. Surely you must have learned something. Do what the customs openers do. Get your hook under the steel bands with a chock of wood and stretch them. Then push your knife blade under a slat to ease the nails up. Put the chock between the slat and the end of the case and give it a couple of taps with your hook to ease the nails out of the end of the case. Pull the nails out with your hook, slide the wooden slat out, and help yourself.'

'You do it,' he said. I did.

He took a bottle of whisky out of the case with trembling hands, unscrewed the cap and took a long draught. His old eyes lit up like stars, and he smiled a rare smile.

'I've never been able to afford this stuff on the wages I've earned in the docks. This Black Label is a lovely drop of stuff. It's beautifully smooth, like Chinese silk. I get a half-bottle every Christmas from my children. Here,' he said, 'try a drop.' He offered me the bottle.

'It's not for me, Dave. A cup of tea or a glass of milk is my tipple. Anyway, I think you've had enough.'

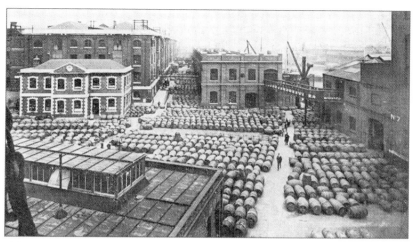

Wine gauging ground, London Dock. *(PLA Monthly, December 1954)*

I was about to take the bottle from Dave's hands and replace it in its case when the lead wheelbarrowman came into the rail truck. Dave went deadly pale. We loaded six cases of Scotch onto the wheelbarrow and the trucker hurried off at speed.

'Holy Mary!' said Dave, who was a Roman Catholic. 'The Port Authority Police will be round here in a few minutes. Do you know who that bloke is?'

'Yes, that's Turner,' I replied.

'Yes!' Dave repeated. 'He's a police informer. He'll shop us. What shall we do?'

I said nothing, but stepped out of the truck and lifted the running board from out of the doorway to stop the other barrowmen entering.

'Urinate in the bottle, Dave. Be as quick as you can. Fill it up.'

'Do what?' he said.

'Piss in the damn thing, you silly old sod!'

'Oh! Right!'

He did as I asked him, but he was shaking like a leaf on a tree in a high wind.

'That will look more like a bottle of bloody cocktail than a bottle of whisky by the time you've finished with it,' I said. 'For Christ's sake, give me the bottle.'

I took the bottle off him, replaced the screw top, then ran my gloved hands over it to remove any prints, placed it back in its case and nailed the slat back into position. I then turned the case over, put the point of my hook in between the steel bands and turned it to tighten them. I hurriedly jumped out of the rail truck and replaced the running board so the barrowmen could enter. I put the broached case of whisky on the top of the next barrowload of cases. All this action went on while Old Dave just stood where he was, rooted to the spot. He was as stiff as a tailor's dummy, and more scared than a rabbit. It didn't help matters when I quipped, 'We could get six months for this.'

'Do you know who it is Turner reports to?' he said. 'It's that copper they call the Red Cap. You know, that bloke who the lads say served in the Military Police during the last war. He's a really nasty piece of work; he acts as though he's still in the army; he'll turn this place upside down when he gets here.'

Of course, I had to laugh. 'Good luck to him, Dave,' I said. 'He'll have his work cut out. Let's hope he doesn't find the only warm bottle in the consignment.'

'What do you mean?' he said.

I smiled and winked at him, 'You work it out, Dave,' I told him.

When the next wheelbarrowman came into the truck I said, 'I'll take this set for you, Charlie. You can give Dave a hand loading up while I'm away. I've got to go to the toilet.'

Charlie must have known something was wrong. There wasn't a toilet within a quarter of a mile, but he kept quiet, took my hook and helped Dave load my barrow.

I set off, pushing the wheelbarrow with six cases of whisky which I took straight into the warehouse lock-up. I had to pass a HM Customs watcher, who had a key to the lock-up where the whisky was being stored till shipment, and the receiving clerk, who was tallying the cases as the barrowmen went past him. When I got to the stowage I pushed the set up against the existing stacks, took the broached case off the barrow I had just brought in and put it several tiers further along the stowage. I walked out of the lock-up and left the barrow by the customs watcher. I jokingly asked him to keep an eye on it till I came back from the toilet. Then I quickly made my way back to the rail truck and told Charlie to collect his barrow from outside the lock-up.

I had hardly arrived back to help Dave load the next barrow when a Port Authority Police car arrived carrying the Red Cap and one other, a bloke I had never seen before. The two of them walked quickly along the freight-striking bank at the back of the transit shed. They looked in the rail truck we were working. The Red Cap glared at Dave and me but said nothing. He walked up to the customs watcher and whispered something, then went to the receiving clerk. The Red Cap took the tally sheet and looked down it.

'Where is the break in the number of barrowmen?' he asked the clerk.

'What do you mean?' was the reply.

'When they went from six to five.'

'Just there.' The clerk pointed to a spot on the tally sheet.

'How many cases is that?'

The clerk counted, then said, 'Fifteen sets.'

'How many cases of whisky is that?'

'That's fifteen times five, times six, that equals 450 cases.'

'Right,' said the Red Cap. 'I want those last 460 cases weighed.'

'You'll have to get the shed foreman's authority to do that,' said the clerk.

'Then go and get it,' replied the Red Cap.

'You get it yourself,' replied the clerk. 'I'm not leaving this consignment. It's more than my job's worth.'

'Then don't let any more cases into that lock-up till I get back,' he said, and walked off to the shed foreman's office.

He soon returned with the foreman, who ordered the gang to fetch a set of scales and weights. They did, and then discreetly vanished. All of them.

Wine gauging ground, London Dock. *(*Industries of Stepney, *Metropolitan Borough of Stepney, 1948)*

'There you are,' said the foreman. 'Now, if you want the last ninety cases weighed, you can do it yourself.'

'Get the freight-striking gang to do it.'

'What striking gang? They've all disappeared till you've cleared off. You don't expect them to stand around waiting for you to implicate them in a charge of pilfering, do you? It's like asking men to dig their own graves before shooting them. But you would know more about that than me. Besides, I'm not paying double handling money on the say-so of an informer, especially that one.' He nodded towards Turner, who was the only one of the gang in sight.

'Are you refusing to help the police in the execution of their duty?' the Red Cap said, assuming the threat might change the foreman's mind.

'Cut out that crap to me,' said the foreman. 'I've got a ship waiting to load out there.' He waved his thumb towards the dock. 'Neither the customs watcher nor the receiving clerk has reported anything damaged or tampered with. If you want the cases weighed, get on with it. Turner will help you.'

Between them, the Red Cap, his sidekick and Turner weighed each of the ninety cases of whisky. Of course there was no shortfall in the weights. If looks could kill, Turner would have dropped dead on the spot. Not because he had passed on duff information, but because he had not reported how the loss of weight in the case had been made up. The Red Cap knew full well he had been made a fool of. He came to the rail truck we were working in. I had told Old Dave to clear off till they were gone.

'Right,' said the Red Cap. 'I know you lot have had a drink. You had better be on your toes because I'll have you.'

'Yes, right!' I said. The Red Cap and his sidekick walked off, got in the police car, and drove away.

The striking gang reappeared as if by magic. It was obvious they had had a drink or two, or maybe three.

'Have you lot been over the pub while this shindig's been going on?' I asked. All I received in reply were some broad smiles and rows of beer- and tobacco-stained teeth.

'Let's get back to work,' I said. 'Come on, Dave, old mate. Let's be having you.'

I put my hook into the bottom of the next set of whisky and rested my hand on the top case. It moved. I lifted it. It was obviously empty. I looked over my shoulder to see all the gang, except Turner, grinning at me.

Charlie said, 'That Black Label Scotch whisky is beautiful. It's like Chinese silk in the throat.' Where had I heard that before? 'It's a pity we didn't know if the Red Cap and his sidekick liked a drink. We could have offered them a tipple.' And they all just burst out laughing, the geriatric, delinquent old sods.

But you just could not help admiring them – their resilience, their stamina and their courage. They had fought and won wars, they had worked as wage slaves all their lives, and they surely deserved their tipple of Black Label (smooth as Chinese silk), God bless them.

16

'RATS, RATS, AS FAT AS TABBY CATS'

She was a South American-registered whaling ship docked on Tilbury Riverside jetty, towed into her berth by the old Thames steam tug *Tanga*. She had docked to discharge a cargo of whale meal and meat. Just because the vessel I am writing about was a South American-registered ship, that does not mean she was owned by a South American shipping company. It was more than possible she was sailing under a flag of convenience and that her true owner was either Japanese or Norwegian. The trick of registering ships under a flag of convenience was used for a number of purposes, possibly tax evasion, or the employment of non-unionized, unskilled crews, or in the cases of whaling ships, to obtain a larger quota of the whale catch permitted under an international law that was designed to prevent the species being hunted into extinction.

She was a large vessel, this South American whaler. She not only acted as the mother ship to the whaling boat crews who pursued and caught the animals, but also had all the facilities to winch the catch onto her deck, dissect them, boil down the blubber to extract the oil (which was filtered into large tanks below decks), and to cut up excess meat and grind down the waste flesh into meal (which was used as a fertilizer in horticulture and as a feed stock for animals and fish). The oil extracted from the thick layers of fat under the animals' skin (and also from sperm whales' heads) was used in the manufacture of candles, margarine, soap and numerous other products.

Whaling was, and still is, a very distasteful industry. But, like every creature on God's earth, when they have been caught, killed, butchered, rendered down and put in second-hand hessian sacks, whales don't look very big. They look at their worst, however, when their bagged remains are teeming with rats. Yes, big, fat, black rats, each one bloated out with whale meat that had been washed into the scuppers and various other places along and below the ship's deck.

The rats had made nests in the whale meal, which not only provided them with good food but also furnished them with comfortable, warm surroundings in which to mate and breed. In fact, below decks and among the whale meal cargo the environment was nothing if not a rats' paradise. It was a proverbial Garden of Eden. It was a haven and a heaven for rats. The Pied Piper of Hamelin could have had a field day piping the vermin into the sea. But alas, for the rats, it was the dockers of Tilbury who were to bring an end to their fabulously rich, man-created, ideal world by the simple expedient of transferring their habitat from the warm comfort of the whaling ship's bosom into battered, weather-stained, cold, steel barges – barges that were lying like predators' offspring, patiently waiting to receive and devour the whale meal regurgitated from their parents.

It had been noticed by a few of the more enlightened dockers – those who took the trouble to go into the local library to read Lloyd's List of Shipping, that is – that a whaling ship was due to arrive in the Thames, bound for Tilbury Docks, on a particular date. The discharging piecework rate for whale meal and meat was listed in the Port of London Ocean Trades PieceWork Rates price book as 3s and 6½d per ton per twelve-handed ship's gang, working over-side into barges on 1-hundredweight bags. But because these commodities were mainly stowed in confined lazaret hatches and bobby hatches, it was often possible to obtain extra payments to compensate for the slowness of discharging the cargo and the extra physical effort involved in carrying the bags from under the deck spaces. There were also potential extra payments for other contingencies. I should mention here that whale factory ships stank to high heaven. It is hard to describe such a stench. One can only say it was the smell of the death of whales. However, the working conditions were paid in with the discharging rate of the freight. So the dockers had to put up with the stench for no extra payment.

Because whaling was a seasonal trade, when a whaler came into port stevedoring labour contractors were employed by the ship's owners to service her. Dockers would be picked up in the Dock Labour Board compounds (or, in the case of stevedores, on the cobblestones outside the docks) to man the ship under the authority of a ship worker. Invariably the vessel would already be alongside its berth, ready to begin discharging its cargo, when the ship's gangs appeared on the scene. Lightermen would have barges moored to the ship's side, scraping their vessel's plates on the over-side of the ship, waiting to receive the discharged freight by means of the ship's derricks. Or they would have barges tied to the shore side of the jetty to receive the cargo by crane. OST clerks would be standing by, one assigned to each gang, to take separate tallies of the discharging cargoes for each ship's gang. The gangs, when they came aboard the ship, would remove the covers and beams from the main hatches, the lazaret and bobby hatches. Hemp ropes, to be used in the discharging operations, were bought aboard by crane or the ship's purchase. It was then that the real fun began.

'What are all those bright little lights down there?' said Les. The gang were standing round the hatch opening.

'Bits of whale bone that have come out of the sacks, I suppose,' replied Tom as he jumped down onto the sacks of whale meal.

'Whale bone, my arse,' said Les. 'They have all disappeared now.'

'Rats! They're bloody rats,' said old Percy, the top hand. 'That lazaret's full of them. You can't see any dead ones, can you? Those things carry the bubonic plague.'

'What do you know about rats and bubonic plague, you silly old sod?' one of the gang teased Percy.

'If you had been in the trenches during the First World War, sonny,' old Percy replied, 'you would know what I mean about rats. The trenches and battlefields

were running alive with the vermin. We soldiers used to sing a song about them –
"There are rats, rats, as fat as tabby cats, in the stores, in the stores. There are
rats, rats, as big as tabby cats, in the quartermaster's stores".'

'Cut that out, you lot. Are we going to start work today?' Bill, the down-hold
foreman, broke into the conversation. 'Stop your gassing and throw those ropes
down into the hatch. There isn't enough room for all of us to get down there. Any
two of you break into the stowage in that bobby hatch, while the rest of us break
into this lazaret. Go on. Get moving.'

The gang worked from 8 a.m. till 9.30 a.m., when a Port Authority mobile tea
van came on the scene. Then they clambered out of the holds, lazarets, bobby
hatches and barges and made their way off the jetty by means of a steel catwalk.
They were smothered in whale meal, which was sticking to them where they had
been sweating in the form of a greyish fish paste. Their hair looked as if it had
been dressed in a thick layer of salad cream (or had suffered a direct hit from a sea
gull suffering a severe bout of diarrhoea). They stank to high heaven – I mean
stank like skunks. They stood in a long line, quietly talking to each other, just as
they had done during the war, queuing by the NAAFI or Salvation Army mobile
canteens, patiently waiting for their turn to be served. Doreen, the tea lady, was
not amused.

'You lot look as if you have just been dragged out of a sewer, and you stink,' she
complained.

Most of the dockers smiled, but one remarked, 'We don't smell half as bad as
those second-hand sausage rolls you sell.' Then, 'Are you sure they're *sausage* rolls?'

'We don't sell second-hand sausage rolls,' retorted Doreen, missing the point
altogether. 'All our food is brought fresh from the canteen every day.' That
remark brought a burst of laughter from the dockers. Doreen didn't see the joke.

'What would we do without the tea ladies?' said old Percy. 'They are our single
light burning in a dark room. They are our bright little star shining in a pitch-
black heaven.' Then, on a more serious note, he said, 'If they weren't here to nag
us during the day, we'd be out of practice for a good nagging when we get back
home at night. We should count our blessings while we may. Come on, my team.
Let's get back to work.'

We walked slowly, but purposefully, back up the catwalk onto the jetty, then
onto the ship's gangway, which descended to the deck. We gathered round the
lazaret from which a thousand tiny diamonds of light were sparkling.

'Bloody hell! What are they?' said Les.

'Rats,' said old Percy. 'I told you. There are millions of them.'

'Yes! We know! You had them in the trenches and on the battlefields in the
First World War.'

'Are you lot going back to work?' said Bill, in his authoritative foreman's voice.

'I'm not going down there,' said Les. 'Let's get the Governor here and ask for a
price to do the job.'

After a short discussion among the gang, confirming the intention to wait for
the Governor to turn up and appraise the job, the down-hold foreman
approached the ship worker to explain about the rats. The ship worker was
already aware of the problem after complaints from the other gangs on the ship.

'I've sent for the Governor,' he said, 'but you know what he's like. He won't turn up till the last gang has stopped work. Then he'll accuse you of being on strike and call in your union officer to negotiate. He won't offer you anything for the job. He'll say it's normal working. You may as well get back to work.'

'We had better wait for the Governor to turn up,' said Bill. 'Get the decision straight from the horse's mouth. Otherwise the lads will think I'm selling them down the river.'

'OK,' said the ship worker, 'have it your own way.'

As other gangs broke into their stowages in the various cargo holds on the ship, they, too, discovered rats were in residence. They, too, concluded they were entitled to something more than 3½d per ton per man – especially after they had been advised by old Percy that they could catch bubonic plague or Weil's disease, or both, from the rats. It was not long before the work on discharging came to an abrupt stop. Then the Governor finally condescended to put in an appearance.

The Governor was an Oxford University graduate, a man who had worked his way up to be the docks manager of the labour stevedoring company that had been contracted to discharge the cargo from this South American whaling vessel. He had achieved his exalted position by the simple tactic of marrying the president of the company's daughter – a sneaky, remunerative move into the higher echelons of the stevedoring and docking industry, and without his having to learn the facts about ships.

These are quite simple facts. For example, the stern is at the back and the bow is at the front and the keel runs along the bottom of a ship; the steel poles sticking up out of the deck are called derricks, and the drums revolving forwards and backwards are winch drums, implements used to raise and lower loads of cargo; those tall, mechanical monsters straddling the quayside are cranes; those rag-clad characters standing about the ship's deck covered in whale meal and sweat are men, human beings – a fact he never appeared, or wished, to understand. To him they were cannon fodder in wartime and wage slaves in peacetime. He was, in fact, through his upbringing and education, a social psychopath with megalomaniac tendencies that were solely derived from his exalted position within the port transport industry.

The dockers, looking down at the perimeter road from the whaler's deck, saw the Governor's car pull up. They watched as he got out and closed the door. They watched as he took his pipe and tobacco pouch out of his pocket and lit up with cool slow deliberation. (This act was contrary to Port Authority by-laws with a maximum fine of £2. But that law was used only for prosecuting the ordinary workers in the Docklands. People like the Governor were exempt from such punishment.) They saw the jetty office door open and the ship worker come out to join him. They watched as the two men moved up the catwalk onto the jetty then onto the gangway and onto the ship. They waited for him to open the conversation, although through long years of experience they were aware of what he was about to say – that is, what he always said when approached by the men: 'Now what's the problem? Why are you on strike?'

A mass meeting of dockers when 17,000 London dockers went on strike, June 1948.
(Planet News Ltd)

'Look down the hatch,' Les said. The Governor looked down the hold then back at Les.

'What's the problem?' he said.

'This ship is infested with rats,' replied Les. 'All those bright little lights you can see down there are rats' eyes, not bloody diamonds. What are you going to do about it?'

'Do? What do you lot expect me to do? There is nothing I can do about a few rats. Most ships carry rats. I've got rats at the bottom of my garden.'

'Have you?' said Les. 'Where do you live? I'll have the health inspector after you. And, while we're on the subject of health inspectors, I think our best bet to resolve this dispute is to call in the Port Health Authority and request this ship should be held in quarantine till it's fumigated.'

'Don't be silly, lads,' said the Governor in a more conciliatory tone of voice. 'I'm sure we can come to an amicable arrangement. Let me contact the shipping agents and see what they are prepared to offer in the way of a price for the job.'

'All right! We'll wait,' replied Les.

The Governor walked off the ship, followed by the ship worker, and made his way to the Riverside jetty office.

'How long are we going to have to wait for a decision?' old Percy asked Les.

'Not long,' replied Les. 'Didn't you notice how much quicker he walked off the ship, along the jetty and down the catwalk, than he had when he sauntered up here from his car?'

'Yes, now you mention it, he did. Why do you think that was?'

'I threatened him with the Port Health Authority. He knew if a health inspector came aboard this ship, and saw rats in the numbers they are running about here, he would send this boat down to the river estuary to be fumigated. That would cost the company thousands of pounds. No. He'll take the line of least resistance and offer us a price for the job.'

'What are we going to ask for, Les?'

'Well, what do you think we should ask for? Double day-work pay till seven o'clock and our piecework earning?'

'He won't agree to that,' said old Percy.

'Of course he won't,' said Les, 'but he will give us a full day's pay and our piecework earning. He'll go away smirking like a Cheshire cat thinking he's done us down. But there's one thing idiots like him can never come to terms with.'

'What's that, Les?'

'Education is not necessarily a precursor of intelligence.'

The ship's gangs did not have to wait long for a reply to their request for a price to be paid for the discharging operation. The ship worker was soon walking back up the catwalk, along the cargo jetty and onto the ship.

'The Governor's been on to the shipping agents. They want to know what price you lot want to get on with the job?'

'Double day-work till seven and our piecework earnings,' replied Les.

Dockers meeting at West India Docks, 1950. *(Tower Hamlets Local History Library)*

'I'll tell him,' said the ship worker and hurried back the way he had come. He was soon back on board the ship, panting from his exertions.

'The Governor said he's been advised to pay all the ship's gangs single day-work till seven each day, including the last day of discharging, plus their piecework earning. That's the shipping agents' offer. If you don't accept the ship will go to another port to discharge.'

Les called all the gangs together and told them of the offer. He told them they should reluctantly accept it on account of the threat to take the ship away to another port. There were grunts and cursing from some of the men, but a vote was taken and the outcome was to accept the offer. The ship worker scuttled off to inform the Governor of the dockers' decision. The Governor telephoned to tell the shipping agents of the dockers' decision. The shipping agents telephoned the ship's owners to tell them of the dockers' decision. The ship's owners gasped a sigh of relief and told the shipping agents to ratify the decision; the shipping agents telephoned the Governor to tell him to ratify the decision. The Governor told the ship worker to go back aboard the ship and to inform the dockers that, after some hard bargaining, he had managed to get the shipping agents to agree reluctantly to their demands. A few of the dockers were seen to smirk while others among them laughed. The ship worker did not see what was so funny, but he rushed off to tell the Governor that the men had accepted his offer and had gone back to work.

The odd thing was that as soon as the dockers began working in the hold, all the rats scurried off to their own little hideaways. Some of them may have been transferred into the barges with the hessian sacks but, by and large, most must have remained aboard the ship and sailed with her.

On the first day of discharging the whaler, Les called in at his local public house on his way home from work for a quick pint of ale to wash the whale meal down.

'Hello, Les!' said the landlord. 'Are you working on that whaler? Don't sit down! Do you want your usual? You stink like a bloody polecat! Go out in the garden and drink that. Some of the other lads are out there. I hope you won't be staying long. I've got my other customers to think about. I'll have to fumigate this place when you lot have gone.'

'Give your jaws a rest,' said Les.

He took a long swig of the ale, put the empty glass on the counter, said to the publican 'Don't forget to fumigate that', and walked out.

When he arrived home he was greeted with, 'Don't you come in here covered in whatever it is you're plastered with. Take those filthy, smelly clothes off and leave them in the garden. I'll run a quick bath for you. I'll put some disinfectant in the water. What have you been doing to get in that dirty, stinking condition? What on earth have you been doing today?'

'Me?' he asked. 'I've been having a whale of a time.'

IN CONCLUSION

It has to be recorded here that on the day following the work stoppage on the whaling ship several tabloids reported the following story: 'Gangs of dock labourers refused to work on discharging whale meal off a ship moored in Tilbury Docks. The apparent reason for the stoppage of work was a demand that they should receive extra payments. Work was resumed after intervention by their employer.'

17

THE TALE OF THE RETICENT ELEPHANTS

Things have changed over the thousands of years since the Ark was built, and steel ships have replaced wooden ones. I really don't know how much trouble Noah had getting animals to board the wooden Ark, but I can tell you how much trouble we had one November day trying to get elephants off a steel ship, a vessel whose name now eludes my memory after such a long lapse of time.

I have to set the scene as it was when my ship's gang arrived on Tilbury Riverside jetty from the Dock Labour Board compound, and I can only explain it thus. It was one of those cold, damp, foggy mornings down by the River Thames. You know the sort of morning I mean, everything wet from the fog, with large droplets of water dripping from the cranes' immobile jibs, from the ships' derricks, and especially from the ships' wire stays, which ran up to the mast head, and their rat-lines rigged high above.

Up and down the Thames foghorns could be heard, tooting and hooting as ferry boats chanced more to luck than judgement in getting from one side of the river to the other. Tugboats, too, foraged about in the dense gloom, looking for possible salvage jobs or acting as maritime guide dogs for cargo ships that were slowly creeping upriver into the Port of London. Other ships were anchored in the river's fairway, waiting to escape from the port, downriver into the open sea, as soon as the tide began to ebb.

There hadn't been a great deal of work about for some time, and my ship's gang were prepared to take on any job that turned up. As it was getting near to Christmas, continental short sea traders, especially Dutch coasters, were now bringing in manufactured goods and food products for the London markets, much of it trans-shipment freight from the Far East. Although the river was busy with coastal and barge traffic, these vessels were small ships that rarely came into enclosed docks, heading instead to the riverside wharves to discharge. These wharves operated cargo-handling facilities on the river's banks, closer to the import merchants' warehouses.

This meant that any of the large, ocean-trading ships that entered the docks to discharge or load were pounced upon by registered work- and wage-starved dockers, who were ready to do any job that presented itself. That was how our ship's gang

Blackwall Reach, November 1949. *(John Topham Picture Library)*

came to find 'themselves, themselves' – as Paddy, our pro–rata Irish workmate, kept saying – standing about on the cold steel deck of a modern–day Ark.

Paddy was standing away from the rest of our ship's gang, staring up into the eyes of a huge cow elephant, one of the five Indian elephants on board. We were, all of us, at the stern end of a ship that had just that morning run the gauntlet of our foggy river to berth alongside Tilbury Riverside jetty. Mr Dunlop, the Port of London Authority jetty foreman, was discussing with our ship worker, Charlie S., what the labour contractor responsible for the ship's discharge intended to do with the animals that were to be off-loaded. There were some caged beasts that could be lifted off the open deck hatches, where they had resided during the trip from Bombay, and landed safely on the jetty by crane, without causing too much congestion. There they could wait till transporters turned up to convey them to their final destinations.

Unfortunately, however, the Riverside jetty cranes had a safe working load of only 1½ tons. So that would make it necessary for us to break out the ship's derricks to lift the elephants off the vessel. The vessel was due to sail again on the very next flood tide, but the road transport to take the animals on to their destinations had been held up on the A13 by a thick smog which covered the whole metropolis. Also, adding to the problems, the elephants could be lifted ashore by the ship's derricks only when the vessel reached the top of the flood tide. (This was because of the lack of drift, that is, the height of the derrick head above the top of the jetty.) It would have been dangerous, too, to land the elephants till transport had arrived to take them on to the zoos, circuses or safari parks that were to be their final destinations. Tilbury Riverside jetty was open-topped, with nothing but a small linked chain to stop people or animals toppling off it into the river.

Now, as I was saying, there we were, on the stern end of this ship that had recently arrived from the Far East with a menagerie of wild animals destined for public exhibition. Our pro-rata workmate, Paddy, looked up into the eyes of one of the cow elephants and said, 'Holy Mary, have you ever seen such a sized beast before?' Then, turning to Terry, he asked, 'Where did you say they come from, Terry?'

'India, I think, but they're certainly Asiatic,' Terry replied.

'How do you know that?'

'They're far too small to be African elephants; African elephants are almost twice that size.'

'Twice as big as these lumbering great things!' Paddy said, stroking the cow animal's trunk. 'What do you think they weigh?'

'Indian elephants weigh about 3 tons each and grow to about 9 feet in height.'

'By Jesus, elephants must be the biggest animals in the whole world.'

'If you mean land animals, you're right; but African elephants are even bigger than these Far Eastern beasts,' Terry said.

'Bigger?' replied Paddy. 'How much bigger?'

'An African bush bull elephant may weigh up to 6 or 7 tons.'

'7 tons,' said Paddy, taking a sandwich out of its newspaper wrapping and offering it to the elephant. The animal sniffed the sandwich and turned its head away. 'It can't be very hungry. It's turned its nose up at my sandwich.'

'You mean trunk,' corrected Terry, 'and it's not because the elephant's not hungry – it's because there's meat in it.'

'So what's wrong with meat in a sandwich?'

'Christ, Paddy! Elephants don't eat meat. They're herbivores. They only eat vegetation. The African bush elephants browse across the veldt for hundreds of miles, in herds that may contain up to 100 animals. Although they are larger than Indian elephants, they're far less intelligent and far more aggressive, like most animals that live in Africa. Unlike the Indian elephant, they're not domesticated.'

'Do they live long?'

'Up to seventy or eighty years.'

'What are those two things sticking out from the sides of the nose?'

'They're called tusks, Paddy. Tusks.'

'What are they made of?'

'Bone really, but it's called ivory. It's very valuable.'

'Why?' said Paddy, who was still stroking the elephant's trunk and whispering gently to the animal, a practice that brought the comment from one of the gang, 'Look at that. Just like an Irishman. Too mean to make a phone call, Paddy's making a trunk call instead.'

Paddy laughed and replied, 'If you understood animals, you would know how much truth there is in what you've just said.'

'Shut up, you lot,' Terry told the gang. 'I'm trying to explain to our Irish friend here about ivory. Now,' he continued, 'ivory is a very hard substance from which all sorts of ornamental figures are carved – especially by Japanese craftsmen. Ivory is also used for white piano keys, cutlery handles and many other things; in fact the Port Authority has a warehouse in London devoted specifically to the importation of ivory, mainly from Africa.'

'Why?' said Paddy.

'Why?' exclaimed Terry. 'Because the ivory from African elephants is whiter than that taken from Asian elephants. The tusks are far bigger and heavier, too. Some tusks from the big bull elephants weigh up to 100 kilograms or more – incidentally, that's almost equivalent in weight to the amount of forage each of them has to devour each day to survive.' Terry stopped talking for a second or two then said. 'What sort of school did you go to in Ireland? Surely you must have learned something?'

'It was a Catholic church school. I didn't learn notting much,' Paddy replied

'Why was that, Paddy? Were you considered to be too stupid or too thick to be taught anything?'

'I don't know, because the nuns didn't choose to find out.'

'What do you mean? They didn't try to teach you? Why was that?'

'Because I'm a Quinn.'

'A Quinn? What has that got to do with going to school and not being taught anything?'

'Well, I come from a tinker family, what are called "travellers" these days. I went to a Catholic church school, where my schooling consisted of keeping the latrines and classrooms clean. That's all my schooldays consisted of, except for the time I spent in the woods and wild areas around County Antrim with the animals. The woods and wild areas behind the school was said to be where leprechauns lived, so no Irishman with a fear of God ever went near there.'

'What's a leprechaun, Paddy?' George the down-hold foreman asked.

'A leprechaun?' Paddy said in surprise, then explained. 'It's said to be a gnome or fairy in the form of an old man with a wrinkled face; they are considered to be evil. That's why nobody in Ireland goes anywhere near where they are supposed to live. But I found out there were no leprechauns in the woods behind the school, only wild animals. So when I'd finished cleaning the latrines, playground and classrooms, I went into the woods to talk to the animals. I didn't learn anything from my time at the school, but I learned a lot from the animals in the woods.'

'Well,' said Terry, 'schooling wasn't much better for working-class kids in this country before the Second World War. Labourers' children, and those of the unemployed, were given short shrift and were taught in the lower classes of most English schools. But we were taught basic lessons in what were referred to as the

3 Rs, that was reading, 'riting and 'rithmetic, with a fair dose of religious instruction thrown in.'

'Well, I wasn't taught notting, notting at all, except I'm an expert at cleaning latrines, playgrounds and classrooms,' Paddy said. 'How will we get these elephants off the ship and onto the jetty, Terry?'

'Not my problem,' Terry replied. 'Ask the crane driver.'

I'd been listening with great interest to the whole of the conversation between Terry and Paddy – Terry, our know-all university-educated communist ex-graduate, and Paddy our unschooled Irish workmate. After all, I was myself ignorant about the life cycle of elephants, of how and where they lived, and how long they lived. But I was more curious to know how and why they had trunks, so I asked Terry.

'Why do elephants have such long snouts?'

'Trunks,' he corrected. 'Because they've developed them over millions of years for use in gathering forage from trees.'

'Oh,' I replied, 'ask a silly question and get a logical answer.' Then I shut up and made my way ashore to clamber up into the Wellman crane to begin lifting the caged animals off the ship's deck onto the cargo jetty.

I had finished bringing the caged animals ashore, placing the cages in a neat row along the top of the cargo jetty, more or less at the same time as the tide reached its maximum height. By now the Ark's deck was above the top level of the jetty, high enough to get the ship's derricks rigged ready to lift the elephants off the deck and up onto the jetty's top level. There wasn't a great deal of clearance and time was short because the tide would soon be on the ebb. If the beasts were to be discharged off the ship, we had only about half an hour before we lost the clearance required. So I asked the serang (the bosun) to get his Lascar seamen to rig the derrick shore-ways as quickly as he could. Now everything was prepared for the final act of this drama on the Thames in thick fog.

The elephants had been tethered on the afterdeck using chains that were held with shackles to the ship's hatch combing. The animals were enclosed inside a wooden box-like structure to protect them from the weather. This shelter had been removed by the time we dockers came aboard the ship, and our ship's gearer had brought the elephant harness from the store ready for lift-off. Unbeknown to us dockers, the ship had brought with it an Indian mahout (elephant-keeper) and he now arrived on the scene to take charge. There was a problem, however: I spoke no Indian and the mahout spoke no English. So the conversation went something like this: 'You get elephant under union purchase.' No response from the mahout, who just stared at me. I pointed my finger at him and said 'You', then I pointed my finger at one of the elephants and said 'get elephant', then I walked under the union purchase and said 'here.' The mahout still did not comprehend. Fortunately, the Lascar serang was on hand, and he immediately began to pass my orders on to the mahout, who then proceeded to try to get one of the elephants under the union purchase. The elephant, however, had other ideas and wouldn't budge.

Charlie, the ship worker, who had been watching the mahout's antics with the animal, came aboard and said to me, 'You know,' – well, quite obviously I didn't know, so he proceeded to tell me – 'when I was in the desert during the war, I was attached to a Long Range Desert Group patrol who used camels. We had one camel that was more stubborn than all the rest put together. One morning we were going out on patrol and this particular animal wouldn't budge. We tried every trick we knew to get it up, but try as we would, the soddin' thing lay on the sand with its big eyes focused on some object in the distance and it wouldn't move. After we had spent half an hour trying to get that bloody camel mobile, an Arab who had been standing close by came up to the camel, bent down and did something to it. The camel got up and took off across the desert sand doing about 35 miles per hour. "Jesus Christ," I said to the Arab, "what did you do to get that animal to take off like that?" to which he replied in broken English, "I tickled his testicles," to which I replied, "Then you had better tickle mine. I've got to catch that soddin' thing up."' Charlie laughed and said, 'I thought you might like to try that trick on the elephants.'

'That sounds a good idea to me, Charlie,' I said, 'but in this instance there is a slight problem.'

'What's that?'

'Well, in case you haven't noticed, that happens to be a cow elephant.'

He sighed, and then said, 'Then you'll have to go over to plan B.'

'What's that?' I replied.

'You'll have to work it out yourself.' Then he laughed and went back up the ship's gangway, saying as he went, 'If you can't work it out, ask Terry, he'll think of something.'

Paddy, who had been leaning against the ship's deck rail listening to all that was being said but saying nothing himself, now came up to me. 'I'll do it.'

'You'll do what?'

'I'll get dem elephants to go under the union purchase.'

'Be my guest,' I said. 'The tide will soon be on the turn and we've only got about half an hour to get them up onto the jetty. But what do you think you can do that that mahout can't?'

'I'll sweet-talk to dem elephants. Dat's what I'll do.'

'Go on then, Paddy. Give 'em a bit of your good old Irish blarney,' I said. And as sure as God is my witness, this is what the untutored, illiterate Irishman did. He walked up to the first elephant and he stroked her trunk as he began to whisper to her. Slowly the elephant began to turn her head and look down at him. Then, as Paddy held her trunk and continued whispering to her, he started to walk under the derrick's head that held the union purchase, and the great beast slowly followed him while the other four elephants looked on apprehensively. It wasn't a long job for a couple of my workmates to rig the harness up under the elephant's belly, for me to lift the animal off the deck, and for my mate on the shoreside winch to haul it up onto the jetty. Once the beast had been landed, Paddy walked it over to the edge of the jetty where it stayed as if glued to the spot till all its fellows were safely landed ashore. Then, with Paddy still holding onto its trunk and its four companions following, the elephant made her way to the safety of the land side of the cargo jetty entrance. And that's where the animals remained till the lorry transports arrived to take them to their final destination. Paddy stayed with them till they were safely installed on the vehicles, stroking them and whispering to them till the backs of the transports were closed behind them.

Then he said, 'They're very sad, dem five. They told me their friend had died on the voyage over here and had been buried at sea. They didn't want to stay on that ship, but they were afraid to leave it. They were very pleased I was there on board, as I was a great comfort to dem. I hope they'll be well looked after wherever they go.' He walked quickly away.

That was rather a funny experience. I'd never seen Paddy Quinn before that day and I've never seen him since. He just seemed to appear and then disappear. I asked George, our ship's gang foreman, where Paddy had come from. He replied, 'I don't know. I picked him up in the Dock Labour Board compound as a pro-rata man. I'd never seen him before, but he shaped up for a job, so as it was only for a day I took him on. It was a bloody good job I did. If it hadn't been for him we'd never have got those elephants off that ship in time for her to sail out on the ebbing tide.'

'Yes,' I had to agree. Paddy had been more than a great help, but where had he come from? None of our ship's gang had ever seen him before, nor did any of them see him again.

'You don't think Paddy could have been an Irish leprechaun, do you, George?' I asked.

The look he gave me was enough to suggest I should have been locked up in a lunatic asylum.

'Leprechaun?' he blurted out. 'More likely a stevedore from up in the Surrey Commercial Docks. Lots of them Irish up there, descended from the potato famine immigrants. They all still believe in fairies.'

Well, if you ask a stupid question, you can't argue if you get a logical answer, can you? Leprechaun?

18

'IT'S JUST LIKE THOSE BLOODY JERRIES'

This is an odd sort of tale, really, simply because I have to start by explaining why I was working first in a barge, shovelling ballast into ore baskets, then spreading and levelling the same ballast over the lower hold of a P&O luxury passenger liner. The reason was that I was a member of the Tilbury Docks Social Club and rowed for the Tilbury dockers in the Gravesend Regatta. The coveted prize for the winners of this annual event was the prestigious silver Gravesend Regatta Perpetual Challenge Cup for London Registered Port Workers, presented by A.W. King & Company (London) Limited. (The Challenge Cup now holds pride of place in the Mayor of Gravesham's parlour at the Civic Centre, Gravesend, Kent. I think, because it is a relic of a once great industry and is a representation of the dockers and stevedores of the Port of London, the cup should reside in the Museum in Docklands. However, I digress.)

The Gravesend Regatta is an annual event, introduced by our ancestors in the mists of the town's history. Men go onto the Thames (and women, too, in these enlightened days) to row in the same tideways that brought our forefathers to this land. They row for various medals, trophies and prizes. But none of the medals, trophies or prizes was ever more prestigious than the A.W. King cup.

The dockers' and stevedores' race was rowed over 1½ miles, usually on the turn of the tide, in whalers. One had to be fully physically fit to be able to row the course, and as I spent most of my time driving the Stothert & Pitt quay cranes that were used to service P&O liners, shovelling ballast was as good a way as any of hardening the skin on my hands and building the muscles in my forearms and shoulders. So you see, there was a good reason for my annual bouts of ballast-shovelling madness.

P&O luxury liners were, without doubt, among the finest ships in the world. How they were managed at sea I have no idea, but if the attitude of deck officers to dockers and other shore-based personnel who serviced those vessels when they were in port was anything to go by, the Lascar seamen must have had a miserable time. The officers and the deck and engine-room artificers were British. But the deck seamen, dining-rooms and cabin stewards, galley scullions and non-qualified engine-room artificers were mostly from Goa.

A deep-sea passenger liner heading downstream towards the Thames Estuary on an ebbing tide, with a Thames sailing barge in the background towards the Essex shore, 1950s. *(Author's collection)*

Goa was a Portuguese colony on the south-west coast of India, facing the Arabian Sea. Its people scratched a subsistence living by fishing, and growing rice, cashew nuts and spices. The P&O Shipping Company had some sort of contract with the Portuguese government to employ citizens of that enclave as seamen. It followed, therefore, that those men who could get employment with P&O jumped at the opportunity, even though that employment meant they had to carry out the most menial tasks aboard liners or cargo ships; in fact just the same as lower-deck British seamen were obliged to do.

To Goanese seamen, it meant they had to be prepared to kowtow to any order or whim that should be given by the sahibs, that is, officers or petty officers of the P&O Shipping Company. As far as I could understand, the method of employment was that, once aboard ship, the Lascars would spend three months at sea. Then they would be returned to Goa. They would stay ashore for the next three months until their turn came to return to sea in any P&O ship that was changing its crew. Their employment at sea, it would appear, was worked on a rota system. The rota scheme meant that sea-going jobs were shared out over a greater number of men and raised the living standards of a large number of impoverished people in that Portuguese colony. It was a policy that the P&O Shipping Company has a right to be proud of.

However, the pay rates for Goanese seamen were well below those for British seamen. The quoted reason for this was that the wage rates were comparable with what Goanese seamen would have received for work ashore in Goa. But, of course, the real reason was that shipping companies could employ four such foreign seamen for the cost of employing a single British one. It followed, therefore, as a matter of economic necessity that when they were in a country with a high cost of living relative to their low income, the Goanese seamen set up petty fiddles that brought them in extra money. They were not too proud to take pennies, sixpences or shillings. They used the extra cash to buy useful second-hand tools, clothes and sewing machines. They were especially keen to purchase Singer, Frister & Rossmann and Jones sewing machines, which they could buy relatively cheaply to take back home as presents for their wives.

Among the many petty rackets the crew indulged in were selling egg and bacon sandwiches (they filched these from the ship's galleys to order for sixpence each). In addition, duty-free cigarettes they had bought at 2s for twenty on board were sold on for 2s 6d a packet. Cigars, too, that had been purchased abroad were stashed away in hidey-holes around the ships. Such items were kept hidden until zealous customs officers had cleared the ship. Then the contraband would be fetched from out of its hideaways. Furtive little dark figures dressed in their national costume, carrying didi tins that now contained contraband, made their way about the ship or ashore as if they were going to the specially built Lascar toilet blocks situated at various sites on the quay. In reality they were seeking clients to whom they could sell their wares.

One could also purchase 'genuine copies' of Rolex watches for an English pound. They had been bought by the Goanese sailors from the bumboat traders that infested the Port of Suez. Many and varied were the items and trinkets Goanese crews could hide aboard the ship to avoid paying customs duty. I once purchased a pair of hand-carved wooden elephants for 5s. I still have them. They reside in a prominent position on our windowsill, a grim reminder to me of those days long ago when working-class men of any colour or creed scratched and scrounged a living from whatever source they could.

Finally, it has to be pointed out that these nomadic vendors of cut-price dutiable goods generally operated in pairs. One of them, who carried no merchandise, would approach a possible client and obtain a firm order for some article or other while his partner stayed hidden. Then, when an agreed trade had taken place, the two would swap places and the second Lascar would pass over the goods and collect the money. This was their technique for trying to outwit any customs officer who might try to intervene in their business arrangements. Customs officers must have known what was going on, but the trade was so minute as not to be worth the waste of Revenue resources in containing it. (Perhaps Customs & Excise were unaware such rackets were going on under their very noses, but I would not be rash enough to take a wager on that as a fact.)

Now, you may be wondering what petty illegal trading by Goanese Lascar seamen has got to do with the German paratroopers in the title of this tale. Well, it's called diverting one's attention, and such a diversion of attention almost cost me my life. It happened on board the P&O liner *Arcadia*, which was being prepared to go cruising (that is, to take pre-booked passengers on a sea voyage and sightseeing holiday, visiting a number of ports, as opposed to travelling from one port to another).

Cruise ships always took aboard several hundred tons of ballast when they were being prepared for deep-sea duties. The ballast, once loaded, was then over-stowed with dry stores, which were intended to last for the whole period of the cruise. The ballast was generally loaded into numbers 2 and 4 holds. That meant, instead of five gangs being employed on loading freight, only two ship's gangs and a ship's storing gang were employed. A ship's gang loading ballast comprised one crane driver, one top hand (hatchway man), four bargehands and six down-holders. In the case of P&O liners, two pro-rata men were employed to work a bull-winch, bringing the complement up to fourteen men.

A bull-winch is a single steel cable set to run direct from a winch's drum, down into the hold, through a running block attached to a cleat against a bulkhead or stanchion, and on into a heel block shackled to the far end of the hold. By this means, heavy cargo can be directed to wherever it is required to be stowed in the hold. On the occasion of this tale, the bull-winch was to be used to draw full baskets of ballast to the far end of the hold (and of course into other places the quay crane couldn't reach) so the ballast could be spread evenly over the whole surface of the hold ready to be over-stowed with dry stores. Now, the interesting thing about operating a bull-winch is that instead of having just a top hand on deck to direct the crane driver, there are three men on deck: a top hand, who directs the quay crane driver's movements aboard ship when cargo is being loaded into or discharged from a ship's hold, a winch driver, whose job it is to operate the bull-winch, and a second top hand to direct the bull-winch driver.

When ballast was being loaded into a ship, four men from the ship's gang would take turns with the other down-holders between working in a barge loading ore baskets with ballast and servicing the bull-winch in the hold. This meant eight men were working in pairs, filling ore baskets, while two of the gang remained in the ship's hold to unhook the full baskets from the crane. It was the job of the two men in the hold to attach the rings on the ore baskets to the bull-winch hook that would draw the full set of ballast across the hold to its designated stowage. They then hooked the empty basket onto the crane hooks so it could be whisked away skywards and back into the barge for the process to be repeated again and again. Each ore basket was said to hold 12 hundredweight of ballast when full. The average time given to load a basket was six minutes. This work operation continued until a barge bay was emptied. Then all the men working in the barge would go aboard the ship and back down the hold to level the ballast. This operation was known as *trimming*.

As large luxury liners were mostly constructed from steel, they were always deep in the water. Centreboards, fore and aft of the ship's hold, were not necessary to stop the ballast shifting when these big ships were at sea. It followed, therefore, that the bull-winch was not restricted in terms of the directions in which it could be operated. When we removed ourselves from the barge and climbed up onto the ship and down into the hold, we were greeted by a sight that at first made us angry – that was until we saw the funny side of the situation. The two men who had been left in the hold to service the bull-winch were both old soldiers who had served in the Essex Regiment in the North African desert with the British Eighth Army. They had decided to use the bull-winch to make sand dunes. They had made a hut out of ship's dunnage, on which they had written 'Rommel's Headquarters'. They had made several graveyards in the sand with small crosses constructed from pieces of rush matting. They had used pallet-boards to indicate the positions of enemy tanks and left holes in the ballast as shell and bomb holes. Far be it for me to say the whole place was a shambles. The other men in the gang who had been involved in the desert war, after calling them every blaspheming name they could think of, soon broke down into peals of laughter. That's when the incident occurred that could have cost me my life, and they thought that was hilarious too.

While the rest of the gang were swearing and cursing each other over the mocked-up battlefield, I had taken it into my head to change the hooks on the ore baskets. As I coupled the crane hooks onto the rope tail of a basket it shot skywards at high speed, taking me with it. Then it suddenly stopped. Before I realized it, I was three-quarters of the way up the ship's trunkway, about 30 feet above the level of the ballast in the lower hold. The crane had stopped its hoist and the basket was swinging from one side of the trunkway to the other like a clanger in a bell. I had two options: I could let myself be smashed against the side of the trunkway, or I could release myself from the ropes on the basket in which I had become entrapped. I chose the latter option and let myself drop down the trunkway onto the ballast below. Fortunately I landed in a pile of soft sand. It was then that one of the jesters in the gang piped up, 'It's just like those bloody Jerries. Here come their paratroopers.' Of course, the down-holders thought this incident was funnier than the mocked-up desert battlefield, Rommel's Headquarters, the tank positions, the graveyards and all. I didn't.

When I looked up the trunkway the ore basket was still swinging slowly by its tail in the position I had left it when I evacuated myself from it. I got onto the steel ladder that led from the ship's hold to the deck some 60 feet above and scrambled up it as fast as I possibly could. (As a quay crane driver I was used to this ordeal, having to climb ladders several times each day.) When I pulled myself over the steel lip of the hatch I could see both of the top hands and the bull-winch driver haggling over the price of several watches that a Goanese Lascar had strapped to his arm. They were on the verge of making a purchase when I got up close to them.

'What the bloody hell do you think you're doing? Didn't you see me trapped in the ore basket? I was halfway up the trunkway when you stopped the crane. Or did you think it was Tarzan of the bloody apes swinging about down there?'

'We didn't see you,' said the top hand, who was supposed to be the crane driver's eyes. 'We were doing a bit of business with this geezer here.'

'Sod him! You should be keeping an eye on your job. You idiots could have got me killed just now,' I raved.

'Oh, for Christ's sake stop moaning,' the top hand said. 'Do you want one of these watches or don't you? If you buy one he'll let us have three watches for 15s each!'

'Yes, OK. I'll have that one.' I gave the Lascar 15s, put the watch in my pocket and scrambled back down the ladder of the trunkway onto the ballast in the lower hold.

The only comment I received when I arrived back in the hold was from the down-hold foreman. 'Are you going to give us a hand to level out Rommel's desert battlefield those two former desert prats over there have created? If you're not, then sod off home,' he said.

That was the end of that episode. Such idiotic pranks and dangers were inherent in docking. Nothing more was ever said about the incident.

By the way, the Tilbury dockers did win the A.W. King cup at that year's Gravesend Regatta (1959). It was my last boat race before my luck ran out, but that will have to wait for another tale. That watch never did work and it cost me almost a whole day's pay.

A Tilbury dockers' rowing team being presented with the A.W. King Stevedores and Dockers rowing cup in 1958 by the Mayor, Mr J. MacKenzie, and Captain MacKeller. The author is on the far left of the photograph. *(Author's collection)*

GLOSSARY

'A' listed dockers and stevedores men called on for employment by a Port Authority labour master; these men were from all categories, i.e. 'A', 'B' and 'C' registered dock workers

'A' men registered dock workers categorized as being physically fit to undertake all forms of work associated with dock work but excluding crane driving

attendance book book issued annually to registered dock workers that, when stamped by an employer or the Dock Labour Board, registered the number of attendances for wage payment purposes.

'B' man a registered dock worker over the age of 65

backers members of a ship's or quay gang who carried sacks, timber or other cargo to or from working areas

'C' men registered dock workers categorized as medically fit for light duties only.

call stand a raised platform in Dock Labour Board compounds from which ship workers or quay foremen selected their workforce

change-over men pro-rata men employed on ships' decks, cargo jetties or quays to transfer roped or cargo boarded freight from one purchase to another

dabbing on a term denoting an attendance book being stamped by a Dock Labour Board clerk

dabbing concession an excuse stamp given for reasons of sickness or for another acceptable reason for absence from work

day-work money the basic wage payment for those not on piecework

dockers and stevedores registered port workers who belonged to different trade unions; dockers were members of the Transport and General Workers Union (the Whites); and the stevedores were members of the Stevedores and Dockers Union; (the Blues)

dolly-brook a large tent that could be raised hastily over a ship's hatch to protect cargo from inclement weather.

donkey-man an oiler or greaser in a ship's engine room

down-holder a member of a ship's gang working in a ship's hold

fall-back money a guaranteed payment based on the number of 'attendances' proved for each signing-on period in any one week

free call the gathering of dockers hoping to be picked up for a day's work

full-back guarantee monies paid by the Dock Labour Board to registered dock workers who had attended the 'call on' but had been unable to obtain work.

job and finish a payment made by an employer for the men to complete a work operation as quickly as was possible

Lascar an Indian seaman

LDLB London Dock Labour Board

luff a term used when cranes' jibs are moved in or out

measurement rate each item of cargo being exported was measured for piecework purposes and gangs were paid by the measurement ton (although, if the weight of the cargo was greater then the measurement tonnage, then the gang (should have) received the greater weight of the two); Port Authority quay gangs were always paid either 'dead weight' tonnage or two-fifths the measurement rate

NDLB National Dock Labour Board

non-continuity jobs that either were or could be discontinued at the employer's or a dock worker's convenience

OST clerk an overseas tally clerk responsible for checking and recording all freight loaded on to or discharged from working vessels

out-of-sector allocations each dock system within the Port of London was categorized as a sector; men transferred to another dock or port were said to be 'out of sector'

paid off on the completion of a work operation, attendance books were given back to the dock workers, who then returned to the Dock Labour Compound to look for another job

perm registered dock workers who were permanently employed, rather than those who sought work twice a day on the 'free call'

pitch the spot on the quay where the cargo was discharged to or loaded from before being transferred to a transit shed or warehouse

pitch hand men who were members of a ship's gang but worked on the quay, or in barges or Thames lighters

PLA Port of London Authority

pressed men men allocated to work an operation by the Dock Labour Board manager

pro-rata men men, extra to a ship's or quay gang, employed on specific work operations

quay receiving cargo discharged from ships to quay gangs for storing in transit sheds or warehouses

registered dock worker a docker or stevedore registered with the National Dock Labour Board under the Dock Workers (Regulation of Employment) Act 1946

serang Indian seaman equivalent to a ship's bosun

ship worker an employers' representative (always a previous docker or stevedore) responsible for all registered men employed on a ship

ship's gang twelve men (plus 1 pro-rata man if working under ship's winches) who worked together to load or discharge a ship

tick note a chit issued daily to each gang showing the tonnage handled, the piecework rate per ton for each commodity, and any day-work time lost

told off allocated to a work operation

top hand the crane driver's eyes and ears on a ship's deck, signalling instructions to him in the crane cabin above

a turn a 4–6-hour work period

under plumb a point directly under a derrick's head or crane's jib

EAST END MEMORIES
Jennie Hawthorne
ISBN 0 7509 4036 0

Born in 1916 into an Irish Catholic family, Jennie Hawthorne spent her formative years in the heart of the East End, in a truly multicultural community. This vivid account of growing up is told with passion and humour – even though her drunken father struggles from crisis to crisis, and illness and crime are part of everyday life. The author's captivating anecdotes, poignant and entertaining, are suffused by the sights, sounds and smells of the East End in the 1920s and '30s. East End Memories is a wonderful evocation of a bygone age: Jennie Hawthorne's affectionate memoirs will entrance anyone who reads them.

LONDON IN OLD PHOTOGRAPHS
Dave Randle
ISBN 0 7509 4162 6

Judges Postcards have been celebrating the British landscape for over a hundred years. In the nature of their business, photographers have been despatched at intervals in that time to update images and to record changes in major destinations and quiet corners of the realm. The need for current images inevitably created a growing archive chronicling the times before change occurred. That archive has now become a unique record of a century of such change and this book draws on it to present a superb selection of images of London's past. The sheer quality of Judges' photography combines with the author's informative and entertaining commentary to create a surprisingly comprehensive introduction to the capital.

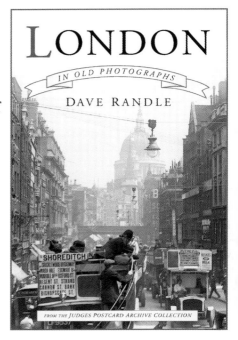

www.suttonpublishing.co.uk
Customer Services: 01963 442030
Email: privatesales@haynes.co.uk